TRAINING FROM THE HEART

Developing Your Natural Training Abilities to Inspire the Learner and Drive Performance on the Job

BARRY LYERLY AND CYNDI MAXEY

Linking People,
Learning & Performance

Ordering information: Books published by ASTD can be ordered by calling 800.628.2783 or 703.683.8100, or via the Website at www.astd.org.

Library of Congress Catalog Card Number: 00-107115
ISBN: 1-56286-144-1

▌ CONTENTS

PREFACE

Maybe it looks like a jungle out there, but nature is sustained through an orderly, delicate balance of many interacting elements: new trees spring from seeds sprouting on rotting logs, predators feed on creatures lower in the food chain, some plants thrive in sunshine and others in the shade of the forest, plant photosynthesis gives off oxygen, which, in turn, supports animal respiration. This natural balance ensures that each species occupies a special niche where resources are available for its survival.

Today's business world resembles a jungle in many respects. As corporations downsize, the pool of available qualified workers shrinks, and more is being asked of employees than ever before. Employees are on their own more than ever, because managers have less time for coaching and hand-holding. Face-to-face meetings are giving way to email, teleconferencing, and voicemail messaging. Organizational changes are occurring rapidly, and employees must be quick to adapt. Trainers are being pressured to do more with fewer resources and to demonstrate results in less time. The heart of the workplace—it meaning and significance—gets lost in the chaos.

Nature overcomes chaos with balance, and so it is, too, with learning. Wise trainers know how to use their "natural resources"—themselves, their learners, and the learning environment—with the same balance and elegant simplicity inherent in nature. The trainer must help learners achieve and maintain balance in the business jungle by modeling an ability to discover answers and encouraging the student to be self-reliant and insightful. Employees and trainers can create learning "niches" by building partnerships for natural learning and, that way, counterbalance the seemingly chaotic, rapid changes in today's work culture. These partnerships must be forged in an authentic, heartfelt manner.

To uncover natural training resources, we interviewed experienced training professionals throughout the country, culled stories from our experience as trainers over the past 20 years, and researched current learning theory and business practices. This book offers guidance, self-assessments, and learning activities to support trainers in their quest to train from the heart. Here we focus on the essential elements for building learning partnerships between trainers and learners:

- the trainer's pivotal role
- a climate designed for self-discovery
- a focus on applying knowledge.

When these three elements are in balance, the result is satisfied learners, trainers, and organizations, but, in recent years, trainers and learners have become distracted by the potpourri of available training technologies and trendy programs. Although these innovations offer some answers, this book shows trainers how to use the most important and most abundant natural resources for effective adult learning: the people and the environment. The relationship of learning leader and learner must remain paramount, the center of balance.

In the first section, "Examine Your Role," we focus on the insights and talents of the trainer. By assessing his or her own style, the trainer can more effectively lead students to self-discovery in the classroom and to a commitment-to-action at work. Learners who are encouraged by a trainer to get involved in their own learning and to make commitments for change will be able to maintain their balance and be successful even in today's fast-changing business environment.

The second section, "Create a Climate for Learning," encourages trainers to identify, trust, and effectively use their natural presentation and facilitation styles. It also addresses one of the most important skills for becoming a learning partner: listening. Discussed in this section are several specific techniques to help overcome emotional, physical, and intellectual barriers to effective listening. The trainer must also be able to ask questions to uncover the wisdom of the learners and elicit the collective insights of the learning team. To generate learning team alignment, the trainer can establish a friendly and collegial atmosphere, create team values, rotate leadership within the team, balance individual needs with team goals, and attend to the physical environment. When the trainer applies these team skills wisely, the results are whole-hearted participation of members, shared wisdom, and application of insights at work.

The third section of the book, "Help Learners Apply Insights," asks the question, "What's the point of training if there's no difference in the workplace?" The natural path leads to application of knowledge and insights, which begins with the learner's willingness to commit to personal or professional development. The trainer can encourage commitment making by building it into the training design. One chapter is dedicated to coaching, an effective means of ensuring that training transfers to the workplace. By establishing balance, establishing learning partnerships, and focusing on natural resources, the trainer will be flexed for the future, in shape to meet the challenge of change, and able to use new types of resources easily. The trainer can use new programs and technology and respond nimbly to changing workforce demographics through marketing and nonstop networking. Taking the steps outlined in this section of the book will ensure that the classroom is the beginning, not the end.

All trainers—beginning instructors, advanced facilitators, training directors, and training managers—can use *Training From The Heart* as a foundation for assessing trainer development needs and for planning appropriate individual development programs. Instructional designers can benefit from the ideas for introspection, needs analysis, and activities that lead to effective training. Also, managers and other employees who train others will benefit from this balanced, natural approach. Parents, teachers, and coaches who want to promote student self-discovery will also find this book useful. To help trainers envision ways to use their natural resources, each section includes "tales from the front" as told by trainers. In addition, we have woven self-assessment activities throughout the book to help trainers assess their personal strengths and identify opportunities for improvement.

Many people have provided support and contributed to our learning as we wrote this book. First, we thank our spouses, Margaret Lyerly and Rob Maxey, for their encouragement, patience, and ideas. We acknowledge the aid of many professional colleagues: Ken Wiedner for providing a framework to rethink the content; Judy Schueler for bringing us together in a workshop; Deb McBride for initial editing; Rita Emmett, Karen Lawson, and Madelynn Hausman for publishing advice; Toni Hupp, Cleo Gray, and Ed Gordon for initial input; and all of the experienced trainers who contributed their wise stories.

Barry Lyerly
Cyndi Maxey
November 2000

SECTION 1.
EXAMINE YOUR ROLE

1 | LEARNING PARTNERSHIP: A SPACIOUS MEADOW FOR LEARNING

Most likely you have been conditioned from childhood that the teacher is the primary conveyor of knowledge. The teacher teaches and the students learn. Students are but empty vessels waiting to receive the wisdom flowing from one source: the teacher. This model has been so ingrained in you that it is difficult to shake. You have probably been on both sides of this equation. As a student you may have met with ridicule or derision when you were brave enough to challenge something the teacher said, and as a trainer you have been encouraged to act as though you were the sole conveyor of knowledge and insights.

EMBRACE A NEW MODEL

That old, autocratic, industrial model of education has to give way to a more democratic model: the *learning partnership*. The learning leader who uses the democratic model recognizes and releases the unique talents and wisdom of students. The democratic model includes the trainer as learning partner. Knowledge power is shared not only for the benefit of the other students but for the trainer's benefit, too. This shared power is what *Training From The Heart* is all about. Sharing power requires speaking and listening from the heart. When listening as a learning partner, the trainer is leading learners by empowering them to share their insights. When you listen in a way that signals to your students that their ideas have validity and worth, it encourages them to continue to share their wisdom.

The learning partnership is characterized by mutual admiration. That admiration often results in the teachers and students reversing roles during the learning process. The late, great conductor Leonard Bernstein was once interviewed on public television about his conducting classes at Tanglewood. He said that he often became the student during these master classes, making the point that great teachers are also great learners. Truly gifted teachers frequently exclaim to their students' parents, "It's a privilege to work with your wonderful kids!" or "I often learn from your sons and daughters." These remarks represent a mental model that contrasts sharply with an attitude of superiority and condescension. Cougle (1977), a great mentor, once said about training, "Remember the answers are out there in the classroom, not in your head."

This trainer's role as learning partner dovetails with a current trend. According to Drucker (1999), as knowledge workers enter our organizations, they want to be recognized and rewarded ". . . by satisfying their values and by giving them social recognition and social power . . . by turning them from subordinates into fellow executives, and from employees, however well paid, into partners." In the classroom, they want to be treated as people who have useful technical, practical, or managerial knowledge to share. The insightful learning leader responds by tapping into that reservoir of wisdom. In fact, the way knowledge workers are treated today is a critical factor in recruiting and retaining them in organizations.

Even before the information revolution created knowledge workers, many experts realized that students often possess unrecognized ability and insights. Bennis (1989) correctly states that, in many instances, students already have answers stored away. He indicates, as Plato recognized, that learning is often recalling information or remembering what is important. By becoming a learning partner, the trainer assumes that students are savvy and wise and uses dialoguing and facilitating skills to reveal their underlying wisdom. Suzuki (1977) captures the spirit of learning partnership in a Zen quotation:

> "Even though you try to put people under some control, it is impossible. You cannot do it. The best way to control people is to encourage them to be mischievous. To give your cow a large, spacious meadow is the way to control him. So it is with people: first let them do what they want, and watch them. This is the best policy. To ignore them is not good; that is the worst policy. The second worst is trying to control them. The best one is to watch them, just to watch them, without trying to control them. The same works for yourself as well."

ASSESS YOUR READINESS TO BUILD LEARNING PARTNERSHIPS

Be aware that when you create a "meadow" for learning, people are often a bit mischievous or at least creative. To point the way toward such a spacious meadow requires attitudes and skills that can be challenging for the learning leader. Are you ready to lead them from the heart? Take self-assessment 1-1 to see where you stand.

Take a closer look at your completed self-assessment. Which natural resources would you like to use more? Which area needs more attention? This book will help you develop your own commitment-to-action plan to successfully lead the learner. The following sections are organized along the lines of the book and provide deeper analysis of the self-assessment.

Examine Your Role

Questions 1–4 asked you to examine your role. The field of training and development attracts many types of people with different motivations, behavior styles, and approaches to learning. Why are you a trainer, anyway? Trainers should know why they are there. Some important self-assessment steps that are outlined in chapter 2 are:

1. Know why you are a trainer.
2. Know what motivates you.
3. Know how your motivation affects the learners.

Self-Assessment 1-1:
Are you ready to train from the heart?

Directions: Ask yourself the questions below. Indicate your level of agreement on the scale, and write your score in the right-hand column. Total your score.

Always	Frequently	Sometimes	Rarely	Never
5	4	3	2	1

1.	I am clear about why I am a trainer and what motivates me.	3
2.	I am educated as to my customer's needs and culture.	4
3.	I know what it means to be a learning partner, and I practice it.	5
4.	I have a personal service motto that guides my work.	5
5.	I am using my natural style to the best of my ability.	5
6.	I am adept at listening to learn before, during, and after training.	5
7.	I can ask great questions before, during, and after training.	3
8.	I can facilitate team learning to promote shared leadership.	3
9.	I know how to help the learner apply knowledge after training.	3
10.	I include a commitment-to-action process in my training initiatives.	3
11.	I am skilled at one-on-one coaching for results.	4
12.	I keep abreast of workplace trends that affect training.	4
	Total	47

Scoring. Add up your points and interpret your score according to the following scale:

60–48	You are using resources wisely.
47–36	You are aware of some resources, but you could make better use of them.
35–24	You need to give more attention to the immediate resources around you.
0–23	You are either not aware of your resources or do not know how to use them.

4. Work to align your needs with those of the learners.
5. Put the learners' needs first.
6. Constantly reexamine the previous steps.

Learning leaders become intimately familiar with the client's needs, culture, and business. You can do this through formal needs analysis or informal information gathering. It is important to use every opportunity for intimacy, from observing how a receptionist greets people to being aware of how employees share their concerns. Intimacy involves nonstop assessment of client attitudes and beliefs. Chapter 3 suggests ways that you can observe and learn about clients' resources so that you can use them wisely.

Learning is simpler when you become a learning partner in the classroom, when you acknowledge that students are savvy and insightful. Even if you possess intellectual knowledge that is useful to share, students are often more adept at applying that knowledge. Too often trainers underestimate learners, using a condescending tone that reflects an attitude of superiority. By using the approach outlined in chapter 4, you can become an effective learning leader who uncovers the abilities of students and acknowledges the balance inherent in a learning partnership.

As a trainer, you bring your own approach or voice to your work. Reflecting that unique style, you can create a service motto to help you focus on the most important things (chapter 5). A motto is clear, concise, and compelling. Your service motto can serve as a compass to steer you in the right direction. It also helps you set a tone for your students.

Create a Climate for Learning

Questions 5–8 of the self-assessment focused on how you use resources to achieve a climate for learning. You have a natural presentation and facilitation style. Experienced trainers learn to trust and to use that style over time, but beginners can develop their natural abilities sooner using the tips provided in chapter 6. First, you can analyze instances when you feel especially comfortable in the learning environment. Next, you can practice specific communication skills such as revealing personal stories, successes, and failures. Finally, you can refer to feedback from sources, such as videotape, peers, and mentors, to anchor your awareness.

Learn to listen, and listen to learn. It is a myth that good listeners are nice. Rather, good listeners are smart. The ability to listen is an underused resource. Trainers who can really listen are the most effective. By following the skill-building format of chapter 7, you can eliminate emotional, physical, and intellectual barriers to listening that affect you in the classroom and improve your listening skills to create effective learning partnerships.

Ask questions to uncover the wisdom of your students and the collective insights of your learning team. Insight and wisdom are revealed when you ask students openly and honestly about a topic. Great questions stimulate the natural curiosity that all learners possess. They provide a link to the real world beyond the classroom. Great questions naturally bond learner and learning leader. Questions send the message that you, the trainer, do not have all the answers but you can draw upon the knowledge and skills of your learning partners. Chapter 8 can help you develop the ability to ask great questions.

Learning leaders know how to develop a team of learners in the classroom. Chapter 9 shows how you can build such a team using certain facilitation skills: listening powerfully, probing correctly, and balancing task and morale needs of the learning team. An effective learning team is like a jazz band improvising: Within a common musical framework, all the members are contributing their unique talents to the whole.

To generate that kind of alignment you need to establish a friendly and collegial atmosphere, create team values, rotate leadership within the team, balance individual needs with team goals, and attend to the physical environment. When you apply these team skills wisely, the results are whole-hearted participation of members, shared wisdom, and application of insights at work.

Help Learners Apply Insights

Questions 9–12 of the self-assessment encouraged you to think about the transfer of training to the work place. What is the point of training if there is no effect?

Chapter 10 shows how the natural path leads to application of knowledge and insights. The classroom is the dress rehearsal for on-the-job learning. Questions focus the learner's lens on after-class commitments. You can enlist existing natural resources, including peer and manager support. The measure of a successful training session is not how well it was received but what happens later at work.

Personal commitment is key to the natural way of training. After all, learning begins with one person's willingness to commit to personal or professional development. You can encourage commitment making and attainment by building it into your training design (chapter 11). Elements of good commitment design include prework, preliminary commitment making, final declarations, and peer support at work. Commitments are pledges to take action in the future. They work.

Training is delivered in various formats, including one-on-one coaching. As you develop rapport with participants, clients, and organizations, they will naturally want more individualized coaching. Coaching, as described in chapter 12, varies from informal exchanges at the water cooler to formal, executive-coaching sessions. The effective coach applies his or her coaching skills with integrity and honesty and assumes that the person being coached is able and wise, not needy and dependent.

The Internet, technology, and the changing workforce have greatly influenced how and when trainers deliver training. If you are truly flexed for the future, you are in shape to meet the challenge of change, and you will be able to use new types of resources easily. You will be able to provide current or updated programs. You will be knowledgeable about how technology has changed delivery and communication in today's business climate. Because you are in great shape, you will be able to respond nimbly to changing workforce demographics, through marketing and networking nonstop. Chapter 13 prompts you to be flexed for the future so that you can consider reinventing your role as a trainer.

THE NEW BALANCE OF NATURE

Breaking out of the old way of operating is worth the effort. The concept of a learning partnership acknowledges that students are more than empty vessels waiting to receive the wisdom flowing from the teacher. The new model flows from the idea that teachers can learn as much from the students as students can learn from the teachers. The result is more self-reliance and confidence for the learners and greater satisfaction for both leader and learner.

The chapters that follow will lead you through the steps to become a learning partner through a series of self-assessments. As you complete these self-assessments, you will uncover your natural ability to forge learning partnerships with your learning partners. They will help you focus on creative use of your natural resources—the resources that exist in your own mirror and in the hearts and minds of your students and co-workers. Through the structured self-assessments provided in this book, you will have a clear vision of how to achieve a natural balance in your training approach—how to train from the heart using your natural voice to inspire the learner and drive performance on the job.

2

DISCOVER WHO YOU ARE

Why are you a trainer anyway? Why did you take this career route? What keeps you there? Often, training and development professionals are so busy developing everyone else that they forget about developing themselves. They forget to check in with their own *why* questions every now and then. "Everyone you know has *whys*, whether they have explored them or not, and reasons for doing what they are doing at work. The *whys* speak to our motivation, our essence, our passion" (Bellman, 1996). What motivates you to be a trainer? Does your personality dovetail with your role? Are you passionate about your work?

Young children have always been masters of *whys*. Imagine the surprise of young parents who thought they had answered their child's query, "Why does a car need gas?" only to have their considered response followed by many more probing, additional *whys*. For children, *whys* come naturally, but it is harder for adults to think about the *whys*.

Adults focus on activity; they become caught up in *dos*. Consider the executive who, after too many 70-hour work weeks, reported in an article on life balance, "I wasn't a human being. I was a human doing" (Baker, 1999). Nevertheless, even human "doings" can ask themselves why. Asking why is a natural place to start on your path to effective partnering with the learner. The beautiful thing about asking yourself why is that there are no wrong answers, only your answers. Bellman (1996) encourages adults to take responsibility for thinking about the *whys*. He cautions, "If we don't think about them, others will. They will assign meanings to our work that may not fit."

It is important to take the time to think and reflect about the meaning of your work. Senge (1990) writes, "Skills of reflection concern slowing down our own thinking processes so that we can become more aware of how we form our mental models and the ways they influence our actions." Reflection is especially important for today's busy professionals. Without it, they tend to become what others want.

Effective learning leaders need to slow down and become aware of their own mental models. In this chapter, you will ask why you are a trainer, what motivates you, where your passion lies, and how these factors affect the learners you lead. You are invited to return to this process throughout this book so that asking why will become a natural part of discovery and partnership in the learning process.

KNOW WHY YOU ARE A TRAINER

Who are you? Why are you a trainer? What led you there? Where are you headed? The answers to these questions affect the outcomes for which you are responsible. Who you are affects how others work with you (your role). Who you are influences how learners learn (the climate). Who you are reflects how training will influence the organization.

Over the years, you have developed a self-concept that comprises all the beliefs and attitudes you have about yourself. You have often gained these beliefs from feedback, and they have been proven in experience. Perhaps people have told you that you are a good communicator or listener. Past managers may have applauded how you organized data or designed projects. Maybe some professors wrote great comments in the margins of your HRD class papers. Others of you may have a favorite childhood memory of playing school. Whatever your feedback and experiences, you have probably selected your work so that it will be in alignment with your self-concept—to make it real. You may have even done this subconsciously.

Imagine being approached by someone wanting to learn more about training and development, and this person asks you, "By the way, how did you get involved?" You pause, think a moment, and then begin to take the eager listener down your career path. You have been handed an opportunity to think about your *whys*! Just in case someone approaches you today, ask yourself a few questions. How did you get involved in training? When did you decide to embark on this field of study? What area of study did you particularly like? Who encouraged you? How did you get your first job? Where are you now? Where are you headed now?

Gerry Waller (1999), a successful performance consultant and training veteran, tells how he became hooked on training:

> "I can still remember my first corporate training experience back in the early 1970s. It was a 10-day training program for the company's new salespeople, and it was meant to orient them to the company, products, markets, competition, and selling strategies. At the time, the company's management considered training to be an important contributor to increased sales and profits, and they had one individual assigned to coordinate the sessions. Despite the poorly designed materials and inconsistent facilitation, the training still achieved great results. I started out imagining the possibilities that might exist if it were done even better. That was the start for me. I took the initiative to learn more about needs assessment, instructional design, training and facilitation techniques, and the measurement of results. I offered my assistance to the training coordinator and helped him structure training materials for each of the sessions. Eventually, I became the training manager for one of the divisions of the company. It was a career dream come true."

Like Waller, many trainers enjoy helping others do things better. Laurie Guest, who specializes in training for eyecare professionals, enjoys the enthusiasm of people who are new to their field. She likes them when they are ". . . starved for information." Bruce Kanarek, who has trained in the employee benefits and credit card industry, considers participation in the development of others an honor, adding, ". . . I find it addictive when I see the lights go on, buzzers sound, and hear the big 'aha.' It's something to celebrate." Debbie Ahlers, a trainer with 20 years' experience, traces her lifelong training career to her teaching background. She says, "I love to teach, be a change agent, and help people 'see the light.' I feel responsible for their learning while also making them feel responsible: It's a team endeavor."

Training and development, as a field, is not particularly old, having its roots in America's industrial revolution at the turn of the twentieth century. It is, however, a rapidly changing field. You are probably called upon to perform diverse tasks. Even the word *trainer* now carries a variety of meanings. In 1996 the American Society of Training & Development (ASTD) surveyed its thousands of members. They listed their job titles in myriad ways:

- corporate trainer
- performance practitioner
- lecturer
- OD specialist
- performance analyst
- training leader
- employee development specialist
- operations improvement coordinator
- leadership training associate
- training sergeant
- continuous learning and improvement coach (ASTD, 1996).

The role of the trainer has changed in other significant ways, too. According to Aubrey and Cohen (1995), ". . . Professional trainers have abandoned the idea they are paid to present, ad nauseam, their products, standing like teachers in front of adults who listen for days on end and then are asked to evaluate what they have learned." The requirements for competency in the role, which have been studied repeatedly over the past decade, reflect change in the industry. For example, in 1988, a study of instructors' competencies by the International Board of Standards for Training, Performance, and Instruction (IBSTPI) revealed that trainers perform the following activities:

1. analyze course materials and learner information
2. assure preparation of the instructional site
3. establish and maintain instructor credibility
4. manage the learning environment
5. demonstrate effective communication skills
6. demonstrate effective presentation skills
7. demonstrate effective questioning skills and techniques
8. respond appropriately to learners' needs for clarification or feedback
9. provide positive reinforcement and motivational incentives
10. use instructional methods appropriately

11. use media effectively
12. evaluate learner performance
13. evaluate delivery of instruction
14. report evaluation information (Rothwell, 1996).

McLagan's (1989) HRD competency study expanded typical classroom procedures to include four major competency types: technical, business, interpersonal, and intellectual competencies. A competency study by the Ontario Society for Training & Development (1995) identified five categories for training and development:

- analyzing performance needs
- designing training
- instructing and facilitating
- evaluating training
- coaching the application of training (Dixon, et al., 1995).

A study of industry trends by ASTD (Bassi & Van Buren, 1999) adds a new set of competencies, which includes systems thinking and understanding, knowledge of interventions, buy-in/advocacy skills, and even coping skills. The central roles for trainers are listed as analyst, intervention specialist, change manager, and evaluator. These roles present a contrast to the 1988 study, which was highly focused on preparation of materials, instruction, and the classroom environment.

Take some time now to think about all the roles you play as a training professional in your organization. If you are an independent contractor, focus on your training role with clients. Examine the specific tasks that fill your time. Many of the tasks performed by trainers today are listed in self-assessment 2-1. Which ones do you like the best? Which do you like least? The answers to these questions can help clarify for you why you are a trainer.

Remember that your *whys* speak to your motivation and your passion. As you look further at what motivates you, continue to reflect on your top 10 list. Also, consider those tasks that you dislike or merely tolerate. Do your dislikes present motivational and performance challenges for you? For example, many trainers are challenged by recent trends toward Web-based programming and instruction. Others may feel uncertainty about new learning styles. The first step is to acknowledge how you perceive all aspects of your training role.

KNOW WHAT MOTIVATES YOU

Discovery is what this chapter is about. You cannot lead the learning process effectively until you are clear about why you are there. People are all motivated by different things. Classic motivational theorists such as Abraham Maslow and Frederick Herzberg analyzed what propels human beings to perform. Abraham Maslow's work is most easily remembered as an "energy theory," because with renewed energy people are motivated by new and different challenges. A person's place on Maslow's hierarchy (physiological, security, affiliation, ego, and self-actualization) may change depending on life events. Frederick Herzberg looked at sat-

Self-Assessment 2-1.
What do you like about your training role?

Directions: Listed below are 50 tasks that trainers perform. In addition to tasks, you will find other, job-related reasons why people are trainers. After reviewing the list, circle all of those that you enjoy. Then, review the items that you have circled, and identify your "top 10" favorite activities or reasons.

Activity Category	What I like about being a professional trainer is that I can...	Rank (1–10)
ANALYZE	interpret and analyze data. propose the correct learning solution. provide logistical support, scheduling management. select appropriate methods. select appropriate media. analyze return on investment of training initiative. budget training. approve and select vendor contracts.	6 5
DESIGN	create training tools and media. create training materials. edit/update training tools and materials. design and improve systems. apply skills in instructional design and development. develop job aids and tools. design structured learning activities. learn and stretch. apply theory to practical learning outcomes.	1 2
PRESENT AND FACILITATE	present frequently to groups. facilitate discussions. give feedback to learners. facilitate structured learning, e.g., case studies, role plays, games. help groups gain awareness of their process. listen to group feedback and discussion. encourage learner participation. aim and control difficult comments and questions. manage a comfortable learning environment.	3
EVALUATE	allocate money. recommend performance changes. test a variety of creative ways to enhance learning. design tests and measurements. evaluate conclusions and recommendations. plan future work performance competencies.	7

continued on page 14

Self-Assessment 2-1 (continued).
What do you like about your training role?

Activity Category	What I like about being a professional trainer is that I can...	Rank (1–10)
COACH	work one-on-one with people. give career guidance and advice. see behavior change because of my coaching input. create action plans for learning transfer. help job performance. make a difference in people's lives. solve problems.	4
DEVELOP ORGANIZATION	build relationships throughout the organization. learn a variety of aspects of the organization. help the organization as it maneuvers change. apply training initiatives to organizational change.	10
PROFESSIONAL	have flexible hours. travel frequently. have a good salary. be a part of the HRD field. aim toward another position in the organization. be in an entry-level position in the department of my choice. use my subject matter expertise. have a lot of contact with people. have the right mix of benefits and hours.	9
OTHER	I was assigned this position. I was forced to take this position because _____. I am filling in for a temporary vacancy. Other learning experience for myself	8

Take a look at your top 10 list. What does it say about you? Do you have a concentration in any one category? For example, do most of your answers relate to coaching? What do your clustered responses mean? Or do your reasons relate to professional factors, such as salary, environment, and benefits? For example, does training provide a secure working environment with some travel and a tolerable level of stress? Are you forced to train others? If so, why? For example, many subject matter experts are asked by their managers to do technical training although they have little interest or experience in training.

isfiers (job performance, achievement, recognition, growth, and advancement) and dissatisfiers (job environment, working conditions, salary, security, and personal life). He asserted that satisfiers are linked to the job itself and that dissatisfiers are tied to the job environment.

SHOW-AND-TELL

I *often facilitate a class called "Creating a Motivating Climate" for new supervisors in the credit card industry. My philosophy is that motivation is energy that comes from within a person. Usually the participants agree that motivation is one of the most difficult topics to discuss and to influence. They argue that this is a task for therapists and counselors, not supervisors. We discuss the myths surrounding motivation as a concept, and they begin to acknowledge that, with time and attention, attentive supervisors can indeed create motivating climates for employees.*

I remind them that a motivating climate begins with each of them. Then I take out crayons and art paper, and I give them an assignment: "Draw what a motivating climate looks like for you." At first, I am usually met with puzzled, even disdainful looks, but those are mingled with the smiles of glee from the true coloring artists in the crowd. Before long, they are all working with heads down, crayons scratching, and the smell of crayons permeating the room. There is some giggling as well as some anxious peeking at their neighbors' work. Then we have show-and-tell. The supervisors hold up their drawings and talk about what motivates them at work.

The artwork tells the story. Stick figures represent teams working together well or families at home or bosses who are approachable. Rainbows symbolize upbeat attitudes, flowers express variety, and an open window in the office represents creative freedom. Mountains depict challenges, stairways are career paths, and, yes, dollar signs represent a high salary. Interestingly, almost every drawing includes happy, cooperative co-workers.

Surrounded by the colorful artwork, I remind them that they cannot create positive climates for others unless they have one themselves, and that the people to whom they report can only guess what motivates them. The session closes with a two-part action plan: First, they set a date to talk to their own managers about how they function best. Second, they list ideas for discovering what motivates their team members.—C.M.

What motivates trainers? In one survey (ASTD, 1995), 40 percent of respondents indicated that "a love of teaching and presenting" had attracted them to the field. Another frequent answer was "concern for the human side of work." Many former teachers enter the field for better salaries, working conditions, and greater prestige. Subject matter experts often become trainers by default, because "somebody had to do it."

Some trainers enjoy facilitating a concept through lively discussion. Leslie Rienzie Sculfield, an HR consultant who also trains, puts it simply, "Participants motivate me." Other trainers admit that they like to be performers. One 20-year veteran enjoys helping people learn while entertaining them in some way. Another trainer is motivated by organizing information and creating solutions to problems, abilities that suit his behavioral style.

Others are challenged by needs analyses, interviews, or program design. Some enjoy the sense of fun and being involved with people, and some like to watch the methodical, logical unfolding of concepts to solve a problem. Many trainers like being change agents. They say they like to help businesses improve when their interventions are implemented; they like making a positive difference and forwarding the company's mission through its people.

Self-assessment 2-2 can help you evaluate any gaps between your current work environment and your ideal motivational work environment. How can you communicate with your manager or work team about these gaps? The more directly you can share these thoughts with co-workers and collaborators, the better chance you have of creating the right motivational climate for yourself. Why not take out your appointment calendar and make a note to set an appointment with a collaborator to talk about what you love to do and how you can work together to overcome challenges that prevent you from doing your best?

DISCOVER YOUR PASSION

Is it becoming clearer that you have a particular excitement or passion about certain parts of this training role? Chang (1999) describes *passion* as personal intensity and *passions* as the things that draw out an individual passion such as competition or writing or technology. As you are developing a clear picture of why you are a trainer and what motivates you, you are also uncovering particular tasks or frameworks that you approach more passionately than others. To integrate your passions into your training role takes time. Self-assessment 2-3 can boost your awareness of the times when your life and your work make you feel particularly exhilarated, exuberant, and energized.

Do your passions in life and at work coincide or are they totally separate? Chang (1999) identifies two categories of passion: content-based and context-based. Content-based passions center on highly specialized topics such as drawing, computing, or swimming. Context-based passions center on a theme such as competition or social justice.

In the world of training, content-based passions may involve writing, analyzing data, or public speaking. Context-based passions are competition, unification, or learning. Whatever your passions, they are integral elements of your picture of a motivating climate. They are vibrant colors that shine, just as your enthusiasm and excitement for certain tasks shine before others, especially to the learners. That is the important final step in discovering who you are: being aware of how who you are affects the learners.

KNOW HOW WHO YOU ARE AFFECTS THE LEARNERS

The previous section discussed how your beliefs and values have shaped you as a trainer. You have uncovered your own likes and dislikes, and you know what energizes you in the learning environment. Adult learners also bring perceptions, attitudes, beliefs, and knowledge based on their own past learning experiences

---

Self-Assessment 2-2.
What motivates you?

Directions: Go to your computer and click on that rarely used icon for Microsoft Paint, CorelDraw, or a similar drawing program. Using the online tools and your wildest imagination, fill a page with your conception of a work environment that would motivate you to optimal performance as a trainer. Another option: Get out crayons and paper and fill a page with drawings and symbols to represent your ideal work environment. Then tackle this exercise. Complete the statement in the left-hand column by circling the phrase or phrases in the right-hand column that most accurately reflect your concepts about motivating work environments. Share your vision with a co-worker.

The work climate that is motivating to me...	has defined hours. has flexible hours. includes lots of people interaction. includes some people interaction. allows me to write, draw, develop, or create in some way. allows me to organize, plan, coordinate, or schedule in some way. allows independent thinking and problem solving. allows collaborative thinking and problem solving. has a clear career path in sight. has no clear career path but lots of freedom. includes frequent praise and attention from superiors or clients. includes limited praise and attention from superiors or clients. allows me to sell my ideas to create more income. includes lots of friendly co-workers. includes a loose network of professionals I respect. allows me to present and perform. allows me to research and write. pays a high salary. pays a fair salary in consideration of other benefits. has a fairly scaled salary and good benefits. allows a nice balance of work and home life. challenges me so that I am always slightly stressed and very busy. allows healthy competition. provides a chance to collaborate with a team. other_____.

and feedback. Some beliefs may stem from their childhood; others may have surfaced with the previous afternoon's attempt to learn a new computer software function. Adult learners bring life experience to the classroom, and they are happiest when learning makes sense within the scope of their experience. For trainers, there is a continual discovery process of how to build effective learning partnerships with these diverse, experience-filled adults. Attempting to understand their differences and to adapt to them will make a difference.

Self-Assessment 2-3.
What are your passions?

Directions: Think about the last thing you accomplished *outside of work* that you felt great about, and circle items in the right-hand column that explain why. Then think about the last thing you accomplished *at work* that you felt great about, and circle items in the right-hand column that explain why.

	money
	recognition
	challenge
	pressure
	competition
	acceptance
	friendship
	service
The last thing I did in life outside of work that I felt really passionate about was ___Dancing___, and I think this was because it involved...	*excitement*
	security
	freedom
	independence
	respect
	knowledge
	change
	adventure
	creativity
	achievement
	other___fun___
	money
	recognition
	challenge
	pressure
	competition
	acceptance
The last thing I did at work that I felt really passionate about was ___doing extra stuff___ at the office, and I think it was because it involved...	*friendship*
	service
	excitement
	security
	freedom
	independence
	respect
	knowledge
	change
	adventure
	creativity
	achievement
	other___

THE FIRST-GRADE TRAINER

*E*arly experiences influence adult behavior. For example, one of my earli-
est memories about learning is from first grade. My teacher praised me
in front of the class for my neat desk and completed work, leaving me to
feel both pleased and embarrassed. I felt an inner pressure to do well and to
please the teacher, even as a seven-year-old child. The teacher's gentle and
understanding style, the way she spoke slowly and moved with patience,
bolstered my confidence. But, for me, learning is still tied with achieving,
pleasing others, and doing things correctly. I have accumulated other
knowledge based on life experiences, but I still need to be encouraged to
take risks and to accept failure as a part of learning.

How did this early experience affect my ability as a trainer today? I
continue to be motivated by doing things accurately, but I have learned to
respect people who are not. I continue to listen to allow the right amount of
flexibility in discussion and activities. I continue to acknowledge that not
everyone is energized by achievement and that not everyone loves to learn
in the same way I do.—C.M.

As a leader of learners, how will you reach out to participants? How will you
be flexible? How will you use awareness of who you are, your motivations, and
your passions for mutual benefit? Are you able to put aside any personal biases to
move learning forward? For example, if you prefer structure, can you allow chaos?
Or, if you are on the leading edge of technology, can you tolerate learners' insecu-
rity and doubt in that area? To be an effective learning leader is to be authentic
while constantly aligning and adjusting to the needs of the learners. You will need
to put their needs first, and you will need to adjust constantly.

HELPING LEARNERS ESTABLISH A NEW BALANCE OF NATURE

Richard Bolles, author of the classic career guide *What Color is Your Parachute?*,
was interviewed recently about the changing world of work (Pink, 1999). He
observes, "Jobs today are really seminars. Change is happening so rapidly that
you've got to pay close attention and learn. Today's jobs are essentially adventures.
You never know what's going to happen next." You can help learners establish a
sense of balance in this jungle of rapid organizational change, but first you must
be clear about who you are and why you are a trainer. The guidelines offered in
this chapter can help you build learning partnerships with adult learners:

1. Take responsibility for thinking about the *whys* and other questions. Why are
   you a trainer? What do you like your job? Where do you want to go with your
   career? Remember Bellman's admonition about *whys*: "If we don't think about
   them, others will. They will assign meanings to our work that may not fit."
2. Identify factors that motivate you. What is an ideal motivating environment
   for you? Evaluate any gaps between your current work environment and your
   ideal motivational work environment. Communicate with your manager or
   work team about these gaps.

3. Discover your passions. Become aware of instances when your life and your work make you feel particularly exhilarated, exuberant, and energized. Integrate your passions into your training role.
4. Realize that adult learners bring perceptions, attitudes, beliefs, and knowledge based on their own past learning experiences and feedback and that they are happiest when learning makes sense within the scope of their background. Build effective learning partnerships with these diverse, experience-filled adults by attempting to understand their differences and adapt to them.

Realize that your strengths as a trainer "come from doing the work rather than from some hoped-for promotion, pay raise, or other reward that may never materialize" (Pink, 1999). As you take steps to integrate your passions into your work and establish a motivating climate, you are ready to embark on the next step of building learning partnerships: becoming intimate with the client.

3 | BECOME INTIMATE WITH THE CLIENT

When you become intimate with the client, you can grow a forest from the seeds at your feet; you can learn where your most immediately available resources are, and you can discover how people have adapted for survival and growth. DePree (1990) writes, "Intimacy is at the heart of competence. It has to do with understanding, with believing, and with practice. It has to do with the relationship to one's work." Through intimacy, you can walk a mile in your client's shoes, learning firsthand about your client's needs and culture.

Achieving intimacy is an ongoing process. It encompasses a continual assessment of client attitudes and beliefs that occurs before, during, and after the learning event. It involves a heightened awareness of every opportunity for understanding, from observing how a receptionist greets people to how employees share their concerns. Intimacy may be found in an informal discussion or a formally planned needs analysis. It can be maintained through communication, follow-up and continued assessment. By uncovering the client's habits, strengths, and challenges, you can build effective partnerships to lead learners.

The following methods for building such learning partnerships, though most important before the learning event, can be used effectively during and after the event, too: awareness, observation, interview, storytelling, experience, and shared assignment. These activities take time, but this investment will pay off in the form of a strong, honest learning partnership, enhanced learner commitment, and greater learner involvement throughout the training.

BEFORE THE LEARNING EVENT: AWARENESS

The classroom is where more than 70 percent of corporate training takes place, and it continues to be where trainers daily create meaningful learning environments. The reality is, however, that much more learning happens before, around, and after the learning event. Because of this, trainers need to know how their clients operate all the time—not just in the classroom. Just as a good salesperson takes time to study the prospective customer thoroughly, trainers need to seek out and study theirs.

An organization trains its sales force to be students of their customers. Trainers need to learn to become students of their customers as well. They need to become intimacy experts. Sales personnel know how important it is to gain information about their clients, but sometimes trainers are not aware of how active a role they need to take in this pursuit. This might mean calling people back repeatedly, sending email reminders, or planning ahead several months to be able to attend an important meeting. It might mean stopping by someone's office at the end of the day instead of rushing home. Getting information takes time, trust, and a great network.

Take a moment to think about your very best relationships in life. How would you describe them? Chances are they are characterized by honesty, understanding, and trust. For example, with best friends, there is an inherent trust that allows each person to share both good and bad experiences. Perhaps you can recall a former college roommate who began as an acquaintance and over the years became a trusted friend with whom you have shared confidences, trials, and joys. Such trust does not just automatically appear, but it grows over time and experience.

In addition to time and trust, trainers also need a great network for getting the information they need. This network builds their overall awareness. Star performers at work network ceaselessly (Kelley, 1998). They know who has the answers they need. They know where to go for information and they are not afraid to ask for it. Independent consultants who train are accustomed to doing this, because they have to do it. In-house trainers should also make reaching out a continual part of their work. Lunching with people from other departments is a start. Calling people to compliment them or to ask them about new projects is another awareness-building habit. Networking within and outside of the organization is an essential skill for discovery and partnership.

BEFORE THE LEARNING EVENT: OBSERVATION

Debbie Ahlers, owner of Ahlers Business Consultants, was once assigned a safety-training contract with a large, health product organization. She recounts that to prepare for the assignment, she toured a location that held huge quantities of blood for study and lifesaving purposes. She immediately became linked to her client's mission when she donned the full-body coveralls, goggles, hair covering, rubber gloves, and boots that the employees wore and then entered the large, air-cooled facility to view huge containers of human blood. The wealth of knowledge that came in the simple observation of a facility was irreplaceable. After that, the safety training for which she was responsible took on a life-and-death significance (Ahlers, 1999).

THE WALK-IN FREEZER

A few years ago, to prepare for my role designing negotiations training for a fast-food client, I spent a morning following a store manager around. Never having worked in a fast-food restaurant, I had no idea what went on behind the scenes. I became the manager's shadow for several hours on a busy morning. To ensure that the temperature met the health code standards exactly, we were troubleshooting a possible defect in one of the four freezer fans in the huge, walk-in freezer. It was not until after our third trip inside—all the way inside—the freezer with the maintenance man that I shivered through the reality of a restaurant manager's day. For the manager, this freezer fan detail was extremely important to maintain product quality.

Had it not been for this experience, I might have erred by designing the negotiating skill training to focus only on the customers at the front counter. By shadowing the manager on a typical morning, I realized that her relationship with the freezer maintenance man was just as meaningful as her more obvious relationships with crew chiefs and customers. Would freezer maintenance have come up in a formal needs analysis on negotiating skills? I am not sure. Most likely, it represents an important detail that a busy manager might have overlooked when completing a written form or during a formal interview.—C.M.

Silent observation allows reflection. The senses—sight, sound, smell, touch, taste—constitute our most natural resources for gleaning information.

TELEPHONE WIZARDS

A nyone who trains telephone customer service representatives should listen on the line with them for a day or two. That is what I did to prepare to lead customer service training for a computer hardware company's technical help hotline. Computer wizards staffed the line to answer all types of calls that ranged from the mundane to the ridiculous. I was surprised to learn how much patience is needed to respond to questions that were repeated over and over again. The hotline personnel also had to remain nondefensive with difficult callers. On the telephone, frustrated people tend to use more hurtful language than they might in person. The staff's challenge was to respond to anger in a calm manner without compromising their ability to answer the questions. Sometimes, they were successful. Had I not eavesdropped on these wizards, I might have assumed that customers with technical questions usually asked them in a calm manner. By eavesdropping, I learned that this was not the case, and I was able to tailor the program to include anger management and calming response practice.—C.M.

BEFORE THE LEARNING EVENT: INTERVIEW

A well-known method for getting information before the training event is to interview certain people—attendees, customers, managers, engineers, shop managers, product designers—who can provide information to make the learning event meaningful. Interviews allow you to listen. They allow you to achieve a level of intimacy that results from confidential verbal exchange. They also allow you to plan for the type of information you would like to gather.

Consider American talkshow host Barbara Walters, who always seems to find an intimacy, no matter how brief the time frame or how reluctant the interviewee. She is prepared with a vast knowledge of her interviewee, both as a person and as a professional entity. She models a questioning technique that varies from factual probing to fantastic musing. It is her careful listening that is most intriguing, because her responses seem to take the interview in an unplanned direction. Walters is a master at setting the tone for intimacy, and she gets great information as a result of her skill.

The tone you set for an interview will determine the type of information you will be able to gain. Interviews will typically bring to the surface learning needs that you did not hear about in department goal-setting meetings or other company initiatives. Interviewing may even take you in an unexpected direction. What is important is that it is the right direction for achieving an honest view of your client's situation. Plan initial questions that will allow for a gentle opening into the topic, and be prepared with probing questions to elicit details and examples. For example, you may say first, "Tell me about how the merger has affected the marketing area." Then, be prepared to probe with such questions as, "Has it stifled creativity?" or "Has this challenged your relationship with the sales area?" or "How, specifically, has the merger affected employee morale?"

Amy Maxson, a training coordinator for the National Association of Realtors, was faced with providing professional development programs that met the diverse needs of a hardworking association staff. A series of communications seminars had been offered during the previous year, but class attendance was low, and most classes in the east coast office were canceled. Challenged to find out why, she began the next year with more concerted efforts to get specific responses from managers. She conducted 30-minute interviews with 10 vice presidents and 19 managing directors in the organization who had not contributed before. Consequently, she planned a curriculum that provided topics ranging from real estate fundamentals to effective outsourcing. Attendance grew. Managers even requested mandatory attendance for a few of the topics. People came (Maxson, 1999).

The interview is an important pretraining opportunity. To use it effectively, you must set it up appropriately. To begin, interviews are difficult to arrange. People are busy and sometimes fail to return calls, or they may reschedule appointments. It pays to be persistent. Be clear about your goal and how helpful their information will be to achieving that goal. The interviewee will want to know why you are calling, what your objective is, how long the interview will take, and whether his or her input will remain anonymous.

An interview request might be something like this: "I need to tailor our customer service class appropriately for the operations centers. Right now, it's geared for corporate office employees. Sandy, your two years' experience on the hotline will be really helpful. I'd especially like to know about the difficult questions and the most frequent questions you get. I'd like to schedule 20 minutes on the telephone. I plan to use this information in my general design without tying it specifically to your name or input."

Rhonda Blender, manager of the University of Chicago Hospital Academy, believes that open dialogue is based upon building relationships. At the first meeting with a client, during the needs assessment, she likes to discuss the norms for the relationship—the degree to which both parties will be open with each other and say what they are really thinking. She believes that it is the responsibility of the trainer to model open communication behavior. Rhonda likes to conduct in-person interviews, especially when initiating complicated projects, because she can pick up behavioral cues that can be missed on telephone or email discussions (Blender, 1999).

WHY AM I AFRAID?

It is not easy to be yourself in today's workplace. Sometimes, it is hard to establish an openness or to get clients to tell you who they really are when you're in the information gathering process. However, once you establish an open atmosphere, most people generally love to talk about what they do. The interview process highlights adults' wonderful ability to apply concepts directly to their work. I have never had a problem getting enough information, and I usually have to be careful to avoid going overtime. People also respond to the personal attention and to someone who will listen to the particular challenges. Often during interviews I have thought, "The manager should hear this, too," and frequently, it has been possible to pass on information to solve problems outside the learning event.—C.M.

BEFORE THE LEARNING EVENT: STORYTELLING

Sometimes, in the heart of an interview, you will uncover wonderful stories. The more stories you hear, the more you learn about the unwritten culture of the client. Stories bring the heart into explanation; they touch feelings. A fact long known by professional speakers and storytellers is that stories move the listener from head to heart. Good stories are like precious documents of a company's cultural history. To elicit another's stories is a powerful method for achieving intimacy.

You can use stories in different ways. Some companies use them to illustrate a specific mission. Others actually sell their products through storytelling. A public relations manager for Porsche (Hopper, 1997) once explained, "Nobody buys a Porsche because it's the best way to get to work everyday. It's not a rational decision; you don't buy a Porsche unless you like to drive. It's fun."

To help sell the experience of being a Porsche owner, new salespeople receive a book of stories from plant workers in Germany about how certain procedures are passed down from generation to generation. The book is updated annually and the company goes to Germany each year to get more stories from engineers and assembly line workers in the factory. A typical story describes a German factory worker, who, when asked, "How long does it take to become good at this?" answered, "Oh, I'm pretty new. I've been here 23 years." Another story describes how the Danish highlands' wood that is used in the car is dried, hand rubbed, and mitered lovingly and carefully—just one more factor that sets the Porsche on a pedestal.

The stories serve as a bridge between the salesperson and the customer. Key selling points stem from the anecdotes. The salesperson learns to match the anecdote to the customer. For example, one customer might be most interested in the "race car on the street" aspect of the car; another may be concerned with maximizing quality or learning all the details of the incredible 10-year, rust-protection warranty. The new Porsche owner tends to pass along the stories to his or her friends when they ask why he or she bought the car.

Stories often will come from personal experiences with the product. For example, one Porsche sales training manager (Gilman, 1997) tells a story about how as a child, he got up, got ready, and went to school a half hour early every day so that he could ride in his father's Porsche convertible. His teacher thought he was ambitious even then. Later, he opened a dealership in his hometown.

As a trainer, how can you encourage storytelling? In particular, how can you elicit stories as you prepare for the learning event? You can begin by structuring the interview so that it encourages people to talk about what is special about their work, product, or service. Is it team effort, performance, style, handicraft, or learning from mistakes? Keep asking for examples. Your chances of uncovering a personal story increase with your ability to focus, listen, and probe in a non-threatening manner. Everyone has stories, and a good interviewer with an open demeanor and thoughtful questions can discover them.

BEFORE THE LEARNING EVENT: EXPERIENCE

Nothing substitutes for walking a mile in the shoes of the customer. When you step into the job for a time, you move beyond awareness, observation, and interview into a position as close to the work as you can get. Savvy managers have been doing this for years. For example, both McDonald's and the Disney Corporation have asked managers to take roles on the frontline to gain a hands-on perspective. It is a time-consuming, yet valuable approach. Some schools hold fundraising auctions at which one highly sought-after item is the "principal for a day" offer. Children who have won this opportunity walk away enlightened and appreciative. Have you ever really thought about all the aspects of a school principal's, a mail carrier's, or an assembly line worker's job? Adults learn from experience, and stepping into the role provides the ultimate experience.

Fritz Maytag, the owner of a small (14 full-time employees) San Francisco microbrewery, the Anchor Brewing Company, developed a successful company where everyone does everything. This philosophy evolved when the bottling line consisted of himself, his secretary, the company driver, and two part-time workers. He developed the idea of a company in which "everybody is in charge and nobody is looking over anyone's shoulder" (Gumpert, 1986). The concept of ownership at Anchor Brewery is very strong. Stepping into one another's jobs is a natural experience for Anchor employees.

THE SALES CALL

Years ago, when I began as a training consultant, I did not really understand sales calls until I actually had to do one myself. There I sat across from the prospect's huge desk, my superior next to me, my notes shaking in my lap. I had observed my superior selling many times, and I had researched everything I could find on my buyer, but now I was experi-

encing my first sales call. Somehow, I managed to ask appropriate opening questions, but once, when the prospect responded with a mild objection, I froze. Frantically, I searched for an answer that seemed adequate, but I really had no idea how to respond on the spot to an objection. Actually experiencing the job of a salesperson was an irreplaceable lesson. It brought me very close to the customer. Because of this experience, I continue to believe that role play in training sessions is a valuable tool. Role-playing offers an opportunity to practice what you might say if caught in a difficult situation.—C.M.

BEFORE THE LEARNING EVENT: SHARED ASSIGNMENT

The trainer who is in partnership with the client is aware of the skills, insights, and gifts that learners bring to the classroom. Assuming that learners are skilled and competent, it is then natural to emphasize those existing competencies. By forging a partnership with learners before the training event, you can also create interest, enthusiasm, and even argument surrounding the topic. You can do this through shared assignment.

What is shared assignment? It is shared thinking and preparation for the event; it also represents a commitment to the event. You probably share assignments frequently before events in your personal life. For example, the simple gesture of purchasing a small gift or selecting a bottle of wine before arriving at a friend's house for dinner increases anticipation for the event. It causes you to focus on what is to come and why. What will the main course be? How formal or informal is the occasion? Should you help out by bringing a dessert? You have the opportunity to contribute to a successful evening and confirm your own expectations by sharing the "prework" with the host.

In adult learning, shared assignment promotes partnership through equal trainer-learner attention to the structured learning to come. To develop effective assignments, trainers should be aware of the time element involved, the participants' expectations and needs, and the overall desired outcomes for the learning. This pretraining planning may be the most important design work you do. After all, this is your first impression—your introduction to the topic and your opportunity to establish a relationship with the participants.

THE BENEFITS OF FEEDBACK

As part of a management development series for a large insurance company, I encouraged managers to investigate ways to improve their feedback skills by surveying their peers and members of their teams about the managers' feedback abilities. Through this assignment, managers were able to get an idea of how others saw them. As a result, they were able to focus on individual goals very quickly, leading to an extremely focused session.—C.M.

Time is also an element in designing prework. There is a fine balance between too much and not enough prework. Participants should not be overwhelmed.

PREWORK PROBLEMS

O*nce I attended a conference about adult learning hosted by a prestigious graduate school. The school sent a package of registration papers for the conference with an eight-page prework questionnaire about training philosophies. The time and effort that would have been required to complete the questionnaire was overwhelming, and I finally gave up and arrived at the class with half of it done. So did everyone else. As it turned out, the session was only two hours long, so there was not enough time to cover it all, anyway!—C.M.*

Let the participants know how the prework will be used. For example, alerting them that prework will be discussed early in the session emphasizes the importance of completing the assignment and encourages partnership in the learning. Giving advance notice also helps reticent participants feel comfortable.

Consider participants' needs and experiences during the prework planning process. What is their work environment like? What will they realistically have time to do? How can prework grab their interest without intimidating them? What are their education and experience levels? Will they respond best to a self-survey or something more active and tangible? Will they prefer an electronic format or paper? Will they respond well to the interactivity of an online forum discussion before training?

Once you have assessed the time and participants involved, choose from the various types of available prework. Actually, your choices are only as limited as your imagination and creativity. Typical prework includes self-assessments, outlines, reading, drawing, interviews, event attendance, and personal reflection.

Brief self-assessments, such as skill-level ratings, evaluations of strengths and weaknesses, and measurements of difficulty in certain areas, are commonly used before training. Of course, such instruments can be used weeks or even months ahead as a part of needs analysis, but they are also beneficial for focusing participants shortly before a program. A listening skill check, for example, can help emphasize the importance of a topic that is often overgeneralized in communication training.

Outlines for presentations, such as upcoming sales presentations or public speeches are good assignments to prepare learners for the performance-oriented environment of a presentation skill course. For example, preparing an outline of product features and benefits prepares the salesperson to develop the sales presentation further during the actual training session. Asking learners to rethink a previous presentation is another common way to ask them to prepare.

Brief reading assignments are popular in management and executive development programs. Upper-level participants are challenged by research, current events, and case studies. They can read while they travel. They can read online articles, newsletters, and Website materials. It is important to emphasize that the reading will be discussed and to ask them to formulate a few questions for commentary as they read. Listening to tapes is another viable alternative to help busy employees prepare.

Drawings or graphical representations of a concept can be brought to the session to encourage creativity and to stimulate different ways of looking at something that may have taken on a mundane quality within the organization. For example, telephone customer service representatives can be asked to design the "perfect customer" with water color or markers on art paper. Pipe cleaners and clay are often used in class; why not distribute them ahead of time with a creative assignment?

You can ask participants to conduct their own interviews with managers, peers, or team members to uncover timely topics for discussion that may not be discovered through surveys or assessments. During the session, participants can report their findings. The interviewer role provides them with an opportunity to contribute information about a topic in a safe way. Discussion is interesting because nobody knows what the other person discovered until it is shared in the class.

Attendance at an event requires a very specific time commitment but can help focus the entire group. For example, ask participants to attend a lecture, movie, play, or exhibit that sheds light on some aspect of the topic. Having lunch with another industry's leaders or attending a local ASTD meeting are other creative pretraining activities.

Personal reflections on a topic are perhaps the most personal means of encouraging participants to focus in advance. This involves asking them to think, record, and prepare to share about their feelings about the topic. Journal writing is a popular method that is being used more and more during training. Why not ask them to start one beforehand?

Journal writing is also a great way to uncover learners' feelings. When pretraining activities focus on feelings, the learner is more strongly engaged. Neurolinguistic research supports this notion. Lee (1996), a consultant in mind-body research, urges trainers to make interventions and presentations ". . . as compelling emotionally as they are intellectually." Conger (1992) agrees: "It is on the level of emotions that our greatest learning can often take place and lead to behavioral change." He asserts that learning is more powerful when more than one level of the individual is engaged. Therefore, the added emotional tie-in that occurs before the event can contribute greatly to both partnership and discovery.

The emotional tie-in for the insurance company managers in feedback skill sessions was strongly evident in their answers to this particular pretraining question: "Do you believe that your culture supports open communication of all types?" They responded with stories about their perceptions that stemmed from experiences with previous managers. They wrote about whether they felt cared about, honesty, and evasiveness. Interestingly, everyone in attendance had strong feelings to share, and, consequently, the importance of their willingness to contribute to a feedback-oriented culture became clear.

Shared assignment does not rest solely on the shoulders of the learner. As the learning leader, you should also engage in thoughtful planning (self-assessment 3-1). Ask yourself how you feel about the participants, the topic, and its relevance, as well as your overall strategy for presentation. Acknowledge any shortcomings. If necessary, work to overcome your own barriers to presenting the information or to presenting to a particular group. Be honest about your own level of partnership.

DURING THE EVENT: AWARENESS

Understanding continues to grow throughout a learning initiative. Once the basic design is in place and the first sessions are under way, trainers can continue to be alert to needs for change or reinforcement.

FIRE FIGHTING

While training an entire village staff in a mandatory communication skill class, it became clear to me that the firefighters perceived their situation to be vastly different from that of the other village employees. Though my client and I were alert to this possibility at the beginning and tailored the activities accordingly, the firefighters' lack of buy-in to the importance of communication skills became increasingly evident. Their behavior worsened with each new class. I revised some of the case studies to incorporate fire fighting situations, and I included more fire fighting examples in the content. Although comments on evaluations improved, some negative attitudes persisted.

Finally, I discovered that the firefighters received little or no advance notice of the training; their supervisors just sent them to the training as they arrived at work. They were understandably upset, because they felt that they had limited control over their own schedules and that their time was not valued by their supervisors. Consequently, the firefighters had no time to prepare for or make a commitment to the training. To troubleshoot this problem, which had also cropped up during prior training initiatives, my client and I collaborated to create a quick, easy-to-read flyer to remind the invited attendees in all departments about the classes. The flyer, which was distributed a week in advance of the class, included a 10-point questionnaire in the form of a communication tune-up. Now we had a "no-excuses" approach. All attendees were informed about the training beforehand and would have adequate time to prepare and incorporate the training into their schedules. We realized another benefit, too, because the 10-point tune-up introduced communication issues before the training, helping to establish intimacy with the participants before the event. Intimacy with the participants set the stage before the learning event and continued beyond the initial design into the roll-out of the initiative to keep learning effective.—C.M.

DURING THE EVENT: OBSERVATION

Observation does not have to stop after initial planning.

WHY NOT WATCH?

Midway through a facilitation skill training initiative for an international fast-food organization, the participants repeatedly asked to know more about what happens during meetings with franchise owners.

Self-Assessment 3-1.
Before the learning event.

Directions: As a trainer, think about your past successes in achieving intimacy *before* the learning event. To help you focus, think of a learning event—a specific initiative, course, or group session—and briefly describe the activities you selected to support the methods for achieving intimacy with the client. Why were the methods you chose successful? Rank the methods in order of their value for helping achieve intimacy with the client (1 = most valuable and 6 = least valuable).

Learning Event:

Method for Achieving Client Intimacy	Activity for Supporting Method	Reason for Method's Success	Ranking
Awareness			
Observation			
Interview			
Storytelling			
Experience			
Shared Assignment			

As a trainer, think about your future plans to achieve intimacy *before* the learning event? Which of the following methods would you like to use more often? Is there a particular learning event that would benefit from a new approach that uses one or more of the methods? List your ideas below. Be specific.

Method for Achieving Client Intimacy	Would Like to Use Method More Often (Yes/No)	Learning Event That May Benefit From Method
Awareness		
Observation		
Interview		
Storytelling		
Experience		
Shared Assignment		

Though I had attempted to observe a meeting early in the needs analysis, my client's budget and meeting locations precluded my attendance at such a meeting. In light of the participants' requests, I tried again. Stressing the importance to effectiveness of the training, I was able to negotiate travel costs and arrangements to attend a meeting. Finally, I saw how market managers facilitated lengthy meetings with diverse types of franchise owners. I applied this new knowledge immediately to the next class, and it improved my understanding of learners' needs.—C.M.

DURING THE EVENT: INTERVIEW AND STORYTELLING

One way to publicize what is happening in your company's training initiatives is to report it in company newsletters. You can interview attendees with respect to what they learned and their corresponding future goals. You can ask permission to publish stories that were shared in class. As a speaker, I am often asked to write an article for an organization's newsletter or magazine on topics addressed at a meeting or conference. As trainers, you can do the same thing. Reach out during the initiative to share not only your viewpoint, but those of those who have learned and experienced. Use electronic communication tools, too. You have built-in public relations within the stories and responses of your learners!

DURING THE EVENT: EXPERIENCE AND SHARED ASSIGNMENT

Traditionally, in one-on-one coaching, trainers have incorporated continual assignments; you can do the same thing with groups by building job-swapping and experience-sharing into the training. Ask diverse types of workers to switch roles at some point between sessions and to report their experiences to the group. Homework and posttraining assignments are also becoming more important as work hours become more flexible and classroom training hours fluctuate. Evaluate how effectively you incorporate these concepts into training with self-assessment 3-2. Experience and involvement will keep the learning partnership alive.

AFTER THE EVENT

Too often, trainers' time is so limited that little follow-through occurs after a learning event. Nevertheless, this is perhaps the most important time to remain intimate with your client. You can do some things to increase intimacy after the learning. If you are not able to achieve them alone, you can designate a group reporter whose job it is to provide feedback to you or your department to indicate how the learning is continuing or is being challenged. You can distribute articles to help people learn and grow. You can create email address lists for attendees of each session and contact them. If you are an independent consultant, you can send clients articles that relate to their topics or that would help them grow and stretch.

As for observation and experience, you can commit to continuing both as far into the future as appropriate. You can work with your client to see if anything has changed or if new needs have surfaced. You can also ask your learners to observe and comment, perhaps by keeping journals of how training is being applied.

Self-Assessment 3-2.
During the learning event.

Directions: As a trainer, think about your past successes in achieving intimacy *during* the learning event. To help you focus, think of a learning event—a specific initiative, course, or group session—and briefly describe the activities you selected to support the methods for achieving intimacy with the client. Why were the methods you chose successful? Rank the methods in order of their value for helping achieve intimacy with the client (1 = most valuable and 6 = least valuable).

Learning Event:

Method for Achieving Client Intimacy	Activity for Supporting Method	Reason for Method's Success	Ranking
Awareness			
Observation			
Interview			
Storytelling			
Experience			
Shared Assignment			

As a trainer, think about your future plans to achieve intimacy *during* the learning event. Which of the following methods would you like to use more often? Is there a particular learning event that would benefit from a new approach that uses one or more of the methods? List your ideas below. Be specific.

Method for Achieving Client Intimacy	Would Like to Use Method More Often (Yes/No)	Learning Event That May Benefit From Method
Awareness		
Observation		
Interview		
Storytelling		
Experience		
Shared Assignment		

Shared assignment can also continue into the future, with commitment from both trainers and learners to check in, collaborate, and troubleshoot any additional problems.

PRACTICE GROUPS

he technical trainers in a large chemical company wanted to continue learning about effective presentations after a two-day program had ended. We made initial plans to incorporate speakers' support groups into the organization. Small groups of technical employees would meet over a lunch hour to work on upcoming presentations together, using a checklist provided by the trainer. This plan would work especially well for people who do not present frequently but who need just-in-time or brush-up practice with the skill.—C.M.

BUILDING INTIMACY THE NATURAL WAY

Author Stephen Covey (1989) writes, "The deepest need of the human spirit is to be understood. People are desperate for intimacy." Where does understanding begin? It begins with awareness. A classic plot in books and movies is that of coming home. For example, the grown adult returns to the inner city where he grew up or the newly single parent returns to her small hometown with her children. Returning to your roots returns you to an intimate place in your life. There is a heightened interplay of the senses as you relive earlier moments and trace the path your life has taken up to this point. Your roots are a natural place to start to gain perspective.

As you continue to become intimate with your clients, go to their natural perspective—their history, their roots, and their experiences. Listen to how they grow. Watch how they survive. Learn how they use their resources. Using self-assessment 3-3, check your awareness of tools that you can use for building intimacy with clients. Observation and listening will grant you the understanding partnership that you both desire.

Self-Assessment 3-3.
Getting intimate with the client.

Directions: In summary, think about how you can improve your efforts toward becoming intimate with your clients. Make a checkmark in the appropriate column to indicate if you need to improve use of the method before, during, or after the learning event. Take a few, brief notes to indicate specific ways that you can improve your use of the methods.

Method	Need Improvement			How to Improve Use of the Method
	Before ✔	During ✔	After ✔	
Awareness				
Observation				
Interview				
Storytelling				
Experience				
Shared Assignment				
• Reading				
• Listening to Tapes				
• Web-based Research				
• Article Reading				
• Electronic Chats and Interviews				
• Email Exchanges				
• Self-Assessments				
• Drawings				
• Event Attendance				
• Assigned Interviews				
• Articles				
• Presentation Outlines and Revisions				
• Personal Reflection				
• Journal Writing				
• Articles				
• Support Groups				

4 | Intend to Be a Learning Partner

How do you shift from a traditional, teacher-centered style to a more student-centered, learning partner approach? First, you have to recognize that the pull from the past is strong. You were probably conditioned—as were most people—in the traditional, autocratic, top-down style. Without an honest recognition of this shadow from the past, the traditional role may exert a powerful grip on you that goes unnoticed. Second, in addition to past conditioning, your normal desire for recognition and ego gratification may continue to lure you into the spotlight. The new role of learning partner means sharing the spotlight—literally allowing the learners to become teachers in the classroom. A learning partnership also means replacing some of the gratification that stems from presentation with the satisfaction that occurs when learners become your teachers. This situation is analogous to the satisfaction and pride that a manager experiences when he or she sees a subordinate shine, instead of the ego gratification he or she may have experienced in the past by doing the work alone. To some extent, the trainer and the manager become invisible as their charges take over duties and responsibilities.

What are some telltale signs that you are operating within the old framework? Do you become personally offended when learners challenge your concepts? Some defensiveness is natural when a learner questions you directly and assertively. Your response sets a tone of either openness and inquiry or defensiveness and superiority. Do you listen to learners as a polite observer or as a keen learner? True learning partners listen to gather new information; they do not merely nod their heads politely to acknowledge that the learner has spoken. Do you set a tone for team learning at the beginning of a learning experience by inviting your learners to challenge your ideas? What is your general assumption about learners: Are they able and strong or needy and dependent? Effective learning partners view learners as capable and strong. Are you willing to share control of the learning experience—both content and process—with your learners?

The issue of control must be honestly assessed for partnership to work. Some of these topics will be covered in subsequent sections. To help you gauge your readiness to create learning partnerships, complete self-assessment 4-1.

Self-Assessment 4-1.
Learning partner role rating form.

Directions: Rate yourself on each of these characteristics by using a scale of 1–5, indicating your usual attitude on each continuum by circling the appropriate number.

Openness

1	2	3	4	5

I have most of the knowledge.   I am open to other viewpoints.

Listening

1	2	3	4	5

I listen politely to my students.   I listen to learn from my students.

Dependency

1	2	3	4	5

I assume my students are needy.   I assume my students are capable.

Control

1	2	3	4	5

I maintain tight control.   I share control.

Climate

1	2	3	4	5

I establish myself as the expert.   I encourage dialogue and inquiry.

LEAD AS LEARNING PARTNER

Being a learning partner also implies being a certain kind of learning leader. Most of your learners play passive and compliant roles as they have been conditioned to do. To overcome learner inertia, you need to set a tone of partnership and shared leadership from the beginning of any training experience. DePree's (1990) concept of "roving leadership" is a good way to describe learning partners: "Roving leadership . . . demands that we be enablers of each other." How do you enable participants? One way is to encourage learners to continually share their thoughts and concerns about on-the-job issues. That may mean adjusting your time schedule or content focus to attend to their real-life problems and situations. Greenleaf's (1972) notion of servant-leadership includes the interesting idea that a leader should be *primus inter pares* (first among equals).

SHARE CONTROL TO MAINTAIN CONTROL

This "first among equals" notion reflects the paradox of shared control, that you must share control to maintain control. Nevertheless, sharing control can be a frightening idea. How do you overcome the tendency to exert tight control over both content and process? The first step is to admit to yourself first and then to your learners that you do not have all the answers. You could even admit that they might have better answers than you do. During the launch or opening phase of any training event you should share your philosophy of team learning, shared leadership, and learning partnership. Invite learners to challenge your ideas during your program and promise to be open to their insights. Senge (1990) calls this idea "reflective openness"—the ability to reflect deeply on your own views, inviting others to challenge them in a spirit of inquiry. When you are challenged and you find yourself becoming defensive, back off and remind yourself that you are committed to an open climate of inquiry.

TAKE A PUBLIC STAND

When you declare values of openness, team learning, and shared control, you have made a public commitment to the learners. That kind of declaration enrolls you and the learners in a vision of partnership and shared leadership. Getting alignment and agreement up front reminds all the learning partners of this common ground. When you discuss your values at the beginning of a training session, begin with your commitment to the learners. What are you willing to do to contribute to their learning? One value you may reveal is a commitment to the learners to help them apply their new knowledge in the workplace.

Use a get-acquainted exercise during the launch phase to ask learners to declare their intentions to the rest of the class. Before the seminar, you may ask learners to complete a short pretraining assignment. One prework item could ask participants to answer a question about the outcomes (goals, objectives, or results) they want from the training. As part of a partnering interview process you could have peer partners stand in front of the room and share the answers about what they want to accomplish during the seminar. Public declarations like this do two things:

- Learners take a stand (literally) on what they want to accomplish.
- Each peer partnership symbolically shares the spotlight in front of the class, sending the message that everyone will be teaching during the seminar.

ESTABLISH GROUND RULES

Developing learning team rules at the outset of a training event is another way to help forge learning partnerships. Assigning someone to be keeper of the ground rules helps keep you and the learners on track. Ask the learners to remind you when you break the ground rules; they are for everyone in the room, not just the learners. At regular intervals the "grounds keeper," as one student termed the role, should report on how well the team is adhering to the established guidelines. The keeper is also empowered to interrupt at any time to gently remind anyone who is straying from the ground rules. By allowing learners to share control of the learning process, you are sending a strong message that it is everyone's responsibility to create and maintain a productive environment for learning. You also signal joint ownership of the training event. It moves the context from the trainer's program to the learning team's event. Here are some examples of typical ground rules created in training classes:

- Begin and end on time.
- Listen with respect to everyone's opinions.

- Be open and share ideas.
- Maintain confidentiality outside the classroom.
- When someone strays from these ground rules, be forgiving and gently help the person get back on track.
- Have fun!

Resist the temptation to impose your own ground rules for the learning team if you want authentic alignment and commitment. Let the learners create the ground rules. When they develop their own rules, it takes you out of the traditional role of handling problem participants, because it now becomes everybody's responsibility to maintain a productive climate for learning. Instead of being the sole manager of the learning environment, you have created a self-managing team of learners. You have set a tone of teamwork and shared ownership from the beginning of the training event.

SHARE CONTROL OF COURSE CONTENT

Another aspect of sharing control is familiarity with your content. Once you have mastered the content or leader's guide of any training program, you can become more flexible, innovative, and learner-centered. Why is this? When you are thoroughly familiar with the content of a program, you are more comfortable releasing some of the control. As the famous conductor Eugene Ormandy once said, "There are two types of conductors—one with his head in his score and the other with his score in his head." When you have the trainer's notes in your head, you feel more comfortable becoming flexible with both content and process. You can look out at the learners, shifting from your concentration from the material to the learners, pulling them into the learning partnership. This corresponds to the conductor's ability to look up and out at the orchestra players, and together they create music. The only way to become knowledgeable about your content is to practice, practice, and practice some more. This leads to another learning paradox: You must practice to become spontaneous (Ehrlich & Hawes, 1984).

SHARE CONTROL OF THE LEARNING PROCESS

As you become a more experienced trainer, you share control with learners in all areas of the training process, both content and process. Ask for feedback about your design during a training event. Participants can often suggest excellent ways to improve the way the seminar is being conducted. This includes dimensions such as pacing, exercise design, and time allocation.

LETTING GO

I was conducting a one-day team building program with a group of 30 nurses. After a successful morning session, I indicated that the afternoon session would involve dividing into subgroups to grapple with issues raised earlier by the whole team. Although this idea was in accordance with accepted small group methodology, several nurses objected. They said that they rarely had an opportunity to meet as a whole, and, after all, this a team building experience, right? Resisting my temptation to control the

*event, I became a learning partner in this team building process and
accepted their recommendation to meet as a whole during the afternoon.
The idea of meeting as a whole met this group's need, although I had based
the design on a sound rationale. Earlier in my career as a trainer, I probably would have exerted tighter control and insisted on the small group
design. As I became more confident in myself, my team building skills, and
my ability to facilitate large and small groups, I was able to let go and
share control of the learning process.—B.L.*

PROMOTE INQUIRY

The role of learning leader means modeling skills of inquiry and advocacy. Senge
(1990) notes that people are very good at advocating or presenting positions, that
they are often rewarded for their ability to persuade others to their position on
issues. You probably find yourself in the role of advocate, promoter, or champion
as you present material to learners. You are also rewarded for these verbal skills in
posttraining evaluations. Presenting powerfully is an important competency for
trainers. When you speak clearly, concisely, and in a compelling way, you can
motivate others to act. Nevertheless, overusing these advocacy skills can discourage others from sharing ideas, restrict time for keen listening, inhibit partnership,
and block teamwork.

When you shift into the inquiry role, you become an explorer, using the sci-
entific approach of hypothesis testing. During inquiry you are able to reveal your
underlying assumptions and positions about a topic, and you invite others to
question your assumptions and points of view. When you stay in the inquiry
mode, certain concepts come into play, including the following:

- You know that you do not know.
- You may be wrong.
- You can learn from others.
- You can benefit from feedback.

These assumptions are difficult to maintain when you are looked upon as a
subject matter expert. In many nontechnical classes, everyone is a subject matter
expert. Each person has valuable information to share from his or her own unique
perspectives, experiences, and wisdom. True diversity of thought is possible when
an environment of inquiry exists.

How do you create such an environment? Some of the ways have already been
discussed:

- Create a common set of values or ground rules at the beginning of the
  learning event.
- Share control of the learning event, both content and process.
- Be watchful for negative influences of the traditional trainer's role as sole
  expert and conveyor of knowledge.

What are some specific skills that you can use to create an environment that
will foster learning partnerships? The primary means is modeling a spirit of
inquiry. Telling stories that demonstrate your curiosity and openness to new

knowledge will encourage others to speak up. For example, you can tell learners at the beginning of a new program that most of the innovations in your seminars have come from learner suggestions. You can gather creative ideas from learners whenever you are listening.

LISTENING PAYS

*A*nother trend that works best in a learning partnership is one-on-one coaching. Recently, I was having difficulty coaching a manager who was very proficient in information systems technology. I couldn't get him to open up doing our in-person sessions. I asked him for suggestions on how to proceed. He said that he was more comfortable using email with his co-workers and clients. He asked if it would be possible to coach him over the Internet as well as in person. We agreed to use the Internet medium. This was a new coaching approach for me, so I was somewhat reluctant, especially since he needed to work on interpersonal communication skills. Despite these reservations, using email worked well. The manager was more open using email, which led to more disclosure during the in-person sessions. Listening to his suggestions resulted in a stronger learning partnership and improved the manager's interpersonal skills. This is another example of sharing control of the learning process by listening.—B.L.*

Another way to model a spirit of inquiry is to show that you are a continuous learner. Talk about what you have read lately, what seminars you have attended for professional development, and what lessons you have learned from life experiences. Do not be afraid to share the way failures may have helped you learn. Being open about your own successes and failures encourages participants to be continuous learners, too.

LEARNING FROM A MISTAKE

I facilitated a seminar during my early years as an independent training consultant, but no one would talk during the first day of the leadership program. The participants were polite but uninvolved in the content, despite all my use of small group dynamics and facilitation skills. Finally, in desperation, I asked the participants what was going on. Was it my teaching style? Was it the content of the program? After some uncomfortable silent moments and gentle probing, the participants opened up. The principles and practices in the program were fine, as was the teaching approach. The issue was the president of the company. He used a very autocratic approach, so they saw no practical benefit to the leadership ideas being presented. The president would never let them apply such ideas on the job.*

Had I performed a thorough needs analysis before the program, this problem could have been avoided. From this experience, I learned to become more intimate with such clients before conducting a leadership program.—B.L.

The spirit of inquiry is promoted when you acknowledge that the learners know more about their own industries and organizations than you do. You may be able to share general principles and practices, but they are the ones who apply these in their unique settings. Calling on the learners for examples and insights as you present such material is one way to reinforce the learning partnership. Instead of using standard, selected scenarios and case studies for exercises, create ones from their own organizations on the spot. In the same spirit, role plays are more effective when using content from the participants, rather than packaged information. When teaching interview skills to an organization, for example, it is more effective to use real job openings, forms, and sample resumes than to create mock, generic ones.

TEAM-TEACH WITH MANAGERS AND OTHER TRAINERS

Some of the most rewarding experiences as a learning partner happen during team-teaching. For example, teaching with a registered nurse at a hospital offers several benefits. A nurse can provide more information about the hospital and specialized knowledge of nursing issues. As you facilitate exercises and lead discussions on communication skills, you would be able to combine the best of two worlds: your expertise as an outside consultant and the nurse's insights as an inside expert. The two of you would complement each other and enhance the credibility of the session for the participants. Team-teaching also encourages learners to open up and share their own ideas because "one of their own" is also teaching. By conducting such classes together, you also learn more about the hospital and the special situations facing health care providers. You would also learn more about yourself as a trainer, because people team-teaching are usually comfortable giving feedback to each other about their strengths and areas for improvement. You might also find out that the material you created can be delivered differently but just as effectively—a humbling and insightful realization.

LET LEARNERS GENERATE MODELS

Generative learning design is a very powerful method for fostering learning partnerships. It begins with Senge's (1990) idea that generative learning ". . . enhances our ability to create." To generate means to bring into being, create, make, produce, engender, and derive. Generative learning may be defined as fresh insights created by a learning team. Instead of always providing ideal models, whether visual or verbal, generative learning assumes that learners have the capacity to create their own models.

The traditional, trainer-as-expert approach has the trainer always supplying the model, whether it is the five dimensions of an exceptional leader or a visual image of the ideal communicator. There is nothing wrong with a trainer providing such models for discussion, but another option taps into the wisdom of the entire learning team. This generative learning method provides greater opportunity for building learning partnerships and removes the trainer as the primary subject matter expert. The generative learning design consists of four steps:

- *Reflect.* The individual focuses on past experiences and general knowledge of a topic or issue framed by questions from the facilitator.
- *Record.* The individual captures these insights from reflection.

- *Share.* The individual shares these insights with others on a learning team.
- *Synthesize.* Individual insights are combined through dialogue and consensus to generate a unique team model.

The individual working alone completes the first two steps in this design (the first two *R*s: *Reflect* and *Record*). The last two steps are completed in team learning settings (the two *S*s: *Share* and *Synthesize*).

Use this generative learning design as often as you can. For example: You are conducting a class on customer service. You request that the participants answer some brief pretraining questions based on their own experiences. Specifically, you ask them to recall times that they provided excellent service and about times that they received exceptional service. In the generative learning model, the learners have completed steps one and two (reflect and record). They bring these recorded answers to the seminar. Early in the class, you break them into teams of six to eight participants to reach consensus on the top three keys to exceptional service. They use their individual pretraining answers as their raw data for reaching a team consensus. They have now completed steps three and four in the model (share and synthesize). Each learning team then reports their top three keys to exceptional service, including real success stories from their pretraining answers. There is always overlap in these exceptional service models, which you can point out while debriefing the exercise. Most importantly, these models of exceptional service become the foundation for the rest of the customer service program. As you move to other topics during the day, the entire class builds on the foundational work done during the generative learning exercise. As the learning leader, you have promoted an authentic learning partnership, based on the assumption that the class participants are as capable as you are of generating a learning model.

Whenever you have learners in a two-day program that uses a generative learning exercise, type up and print out copies for inclusion in their manuals during the evening between days one and two. Be sure you use the same fonts and design layout of the manual to emphasize that the answers and models generated by the learners have equal status with your own information. You are now equal partners in course content.

Trainers often use generative learning exercises to encourage participation and discussion, but the insights generated are frequently forgotten as the trainer moves on to the really important material: his or her stuff. You may find yourself falling back into this traditional model more than you would like to admit. Yes, it takes more time and effort to use creative approaches like generative learning to stimulate learning partnerships, but the results are well worth the effort. Looking ahead to posttraining commitment, it is clear that participants are more likely to commit to achieving a model they themselves developed. When learners create their own models, they can see the gap in their own real-life performance. That realization pulls the person toward making a commitment to close the gap. If a learning team creates a model that says exceptional service includes being an exceptional listener, a participant may notice that he or she is often a poor listener when clients are upset. That way, the person is often moved to make a commitment to be an exceptional listener in the workplace. You will discover many learners are willing to declare such commitments to action, resulting in positive progress when they return to report on their commitments.

BE AWARE OF THE PHYSICAL ENVIRONMENT

The classroom environment can enhance or detract from learning. Even though some trends in learning theory (accelerated learning, for example) include lots of bells and whistles, such as supplying toys to relax the participants, do not rely too much on external props. Being a learning partner involves creating partnerships among all the players, learners, and learning leader. If external props, such as music, toys, and wild visual images, continually stimulate you and the learners, bonding may be compromised. The most important props are the human ones.

The layout of the room is also important. Try using a conference table arrangement with additional space for breakout groups. This enhances cohesion when the team is working around the same table and also permits small group processes. C. Ken Weidner (1995), a Chicago consultant, takes the conference table setting a step further. He advocates that the trainer be seated as an equal partner at the table, rather than at the traditional head of the table position that most trainers occupy. All of these logistical matters aim to foster learning partnerships and shared leadership.

ESTABLISH A FRIENDLY TONE

It may seem obvious that you should be friendly from the outset. How many times, though, have you been so busy getting set up or reviewing your notes that you failed to notice learners entering the room? It is easy to do, especially if you do not allow enough preparation or setup time. Developing partnerships requires putting learners at ease as they enter the training area. Take time to greet each person, introduce yourself, and find an interesting topic to chat about. It relaxes both the trainer and the learners.

HAVE FUN!

*F*un *isn't a word I used to associate with my work. Words like serious, committed, powerful, and competent were usually on my mind. When I started having more fun with the learners, learning partnerships developed more naturally. I began to take myself less seriously and to take the learners' ideas more seriously. It also seems to encourage taking some risks, being open, and learning by trial and error. By having fun in the training classroom, my effectiveness as a trainer has grown.*—B.L.

SPACIOUS MEADOW FOR LEARNING

As you shift from a traditional, teacher-centered style to a more student-centered, learning partner approach, you create a spacious meadow for learning. But, to open creative meadows for learners, you must recognize that the pull from the past is strong. You must overcome years of conditioning in the traditional, autocratic, top-down training role. Recognize that forging learning partnerships is not easy. It requires sharing control—from content to process—in the classroom.

Sharing the spotlight shifts you from star to enabler. But the payoff is clear: greater ownership and self-reliance from learners; more dynamic and interactive participation; and a focus on learner issues and concerns. When learning partnerships are created, you become a role model for continuous learning and ongoing professional development. To see how far you have come in the process of embracing learning partnership, tackle self-assessment 4-2.

Self-Assessment 4-2.
Learning partnership checklist.

Directions: Below is a checklist to remind you of dimensions of learning partnerships. Please add your own dimensions to the bottom of the list. Check the appropriate column as you answer each question.

Do you...	Yes	No	Intend to Do More
listen to learn?			
permit learners to teach you?			
honestly assess your learning partner style?			
share the spotlight?			
assume learners are savvy and wise?			
encourage learners to challenge your ideas?			
admit you do not have all the answers?			
declare partnering values to learners?			
help learners generate ground rules?			
share control of course content?			
share control of the learning design?			
promote a spirit of inquiry?			
team-teach with clients?			
use generative learning methods?			
attend to the physical layout?			
demonstrate a friendly presence?			
have fun?			
solicit feedback regularly?			
get satisfaction when learners lead?			
create a spacious meadow?			

5

CREATE A
SERVICE MOTTO

You are driving to work to begin a two-day program on customer service. You are feeling anxious about this first session. Even though you conducted a thorough needs analysis, you are always a bit nervous on the first round of a new course. You take a few deep breaths to relax as you continue your early morning drive. Then, you give yourself a little pep talk: "I am a great trainer!" This boosts your confidence.

Now, you shift your attention to the real reason for your work: to serve your client. You recall your service motto, "Bring out the best in people," and repeat it several times. You say it out loud: "I'm committed to bringing out the best in people today!" When you remember to focus on your motto, your classes usually go better. When you center on bringing out the best in the learners, you begin to fade into the shadows and become invisible. The learners are teaching themselves, and you are merely facilitating their learning. You are leading their learning by providing a context or framework for their success. Your service motto keeps you directed toward what is important and helps you get over your nervousness. It also encourages you to share control of the learning process with the learners.

LEAD WITH YOUR SERVICE MOTTO

As a trainer, you know that managerial functions are important. Managerial tasks can have a significant effect on the success or failure of your event. They include setting up the room to meet the learners' needs, ensuring that refreshments and meals are handled, being certain your equipment is working properly, and remembering to order supplies in advance of the class. Before the learning event, you may also want to be certain any prework has been forwarded to the participants. As part of your pretraining practice, you may wish to telephone each participant. These functions, however, are duties of a manager, not a leader.

Think of yourself, the trainer, as a leader. Leading involves activities of vision and effectiveness. Managing implies mastering routines and efficiency (Bennis & Nanus, 1985). In his classic article on leadership, Zaleznik (1977) notes that leaders focus on philosophy, ideas, and creation of meaning for people. Hickman and

Silva (1984) say that leaders enroll themselves and others in a common philosophy and purpose. When the leader and the led forge a common partnership or share a vision, people have the courage to risk and experiment (Senge, 1990). To lead learners, you must develop a philosophy of training that provides meaning and purpose for yourself and the learners. Chapter 1 discussed leading learners by creating a meadow in which they can play.

How do you enroll yourself and others in a common philosophy? Develop and articulate a service motto. It provides meaning, direction, and focus to the work you and the learners are doing. It provides a context or framework ("meadow") for the learning. It enables a team of learners to align around a common theme.

WHAT IS A SERVICE MOTTO?

A service motto is a philosophy of training expressed in a clear, concise, and compelling manner. A service motto is a type of vision, ". . . a mental image of a possible and desirable future state . . . a target that beckons" (Bennis & Nanus, 1985). A compelling vision is simple, easily understood, clearly desirable, and energizing (Bennis & Nanus, 1985). Such a vision may be either verbal or visual. Self-assessment 5-1 may help you glean insights from a past, successful learning event. Impressions from your past can help you develop your vision for the future.

Corporations have used vision statements for both marketing to external customers and for motivating internal staff. Ford Motor Company's campaign that "Quality is Job 1" served both purposes. Several years ago, a new president came to Marshall Field's department store in Chicago. This new executive, Rudy Hirsch, embraced the past at Field's by resurrecting a slogan by one of the original founders, "Give the lady what she wants," to motivate employees to provide exceptional service. Timothy Firnstahl (1989) developed a catch phrase for his Seattle restaurants, "YEGA—Your Enjoyment Guaranteed. Always." He called it a promise. It became a mantra for his organization, focusing everyone on a single goal. His training, employee rewards, and customer service policies all revolved around the YEGA promise, which served as the focus and benchmark of success. Alfred W. Grube, the president of Grube Pharmacies in Sheboygan, Wisconsin, developed a vision statement that was recited by employees before meetings, discussed during new-employee orientation, and posted throughout his stores. It was, "We are a model of quality and service, treating our customers and associates as friends."

FOCUS ON SERVING

A service motto has some of the same qualities as a corporate mission or a vision statement. One difference is that it always focuses the leader and the led on serving. It embraces Greenleaf's (1972) concept of servant-leadership: "The servant-leader is servant first . . . It begins with the natural feeling that one wants to serve, to serve first. Then conscious choice brings one to aspire to lead. The difference manifests itself in the care taken by the servant—first to make sure that other people's highest-priority needs are being served. The best test is: Do those served grow as persons; do they, while being served, become healthier, wiser, freer, more autonomous, more likely themselves to become servants?"

Self-Assessment 5-1.
Envisioning.

Directions: Select a quiet time and location. Close your eyes. Sit in a comfortable position, and think about a time you were leading an exceptionally satisfying training class. Open your eyes, and jot down your impressions below:

Envision the room, participants, and colors.	What do you see?
Recall the voices' tone, feeling level, and volume.	What do you hear?
Remember your feelings and the feelings being expressed by participants.	What are you feeling?
Recall your thoughts and impressions.	What insights do you have?

KEEP IT SHORT

So what does it mean to serve? To serve means to minister to, wait on, assist, help, or furnish or supply something needed or desired. Besides incorporating the concept of service, the other aspect of a service motto is its motto format. According to *Merriam-Webster's Collegiate Dictionary* (10th edition), a motto is a "short expression of a guiding principle." Unlike some corporate and organization mission statements, it is clear and concise and, therefore, easy to remember. When your guiding principle is serving the learners so they become ". . . healthier, wiser, freer, more autonomous . . ." you are authentically leading the learner. You could shorten Greenleaf's guiding principle by transforming it into motto form: "Helping people become self-reliant."

Here are some memorable service mottoes from seminar students. They may inspire you as you create your own.

- We mend broken hearts (hospital cardiac rehabilitation department).
- Just home cooking (food service department).
- We hear you (communication department).
- Easy payments (accounts receivable department).
- Care for the caregivers (hospital emergency room department).

In each of these examples, something needed or wanted by either the department or the department's customers is at stake. Frequently, the language is emotionally compelling, such as "We mend broken hearts." The manager liked this slogan so much that she used it in a radio interview one week after developing it at a seminar session. She reported a few weeks later that it helped remind her staff of the important rehabilitation work they performed.

The "care for the caregivers" motto is another hospital example. It focuses on an internal need. The emergency room staff was so stressed by the frantic pace and the life-or-death nature of their work that they were forgetting to take care of themselves. Their motto reminded them to be a supportive team and to schedule time to have fun together. The manager of the emergency room also noted that this motto kept the staff focused on communicating in a cooperative manner and on resolving conflicts in a timely way. All that from a simple motto! What a great meadow to play in!

USE WITH INTEGRITY

Using your service motto to lead learners authentically is only possible when your motto is developed and articulated with integrity. This is true for all the methods discussed in this book. Peters and Austin (1985) caution their readers to do the same thing in their excellent book on leadership, *A Passion for Excellence:* "We will remind you in every chapter that each example lives only as the leader's integrity (leaders at every level) lives within it. As you read on we would ask you to stop and pause, close the door and examine your deepest beliefs about people (and their creative potential and trustworthiness) . . . Especially when an idea makes your eyes light up. That's the time to pause . . . Stop, nonetheless. Do you believe in it? Believe in what it stands for?"

When an idea or approach works, as do service mottoes, it might be tempting to use it to manipulate learners to do your bidding. Over time, your participants will see through the fraudulent use of technique. Integrity must underlie all methods and techniques. This implies that you must be willing to reveal the reason you are using an approach, whether it is a service motto or a classroom role-play exercise. Explaining the reason why you use a specific method or exercise keeps you and the learning team grounded in integrity.

DOES IT SERVE THE LEARNER?

When I first became a trainer, I found an exercise called, "Win as much as you can," which always resulted in a high level of group participation and fun. It was designed to demonstrate the need for cooperation instead of competition and was very appropriate for topics such as team building or conflict management. Nevertheless, no matter what the topic of my program happened to be, I would throw in this exercise. One day someone asked in his or her written evaluation why the game was part of the training. The evaluator noted that while it was enjoyable, it didn't seem to fit with the topic we were discussing. That helpful comment made me think about my level of integrity with respect to the way I was using the game. I decided that in the future every device I would use in my designs should be scrutinized by asking: Does it serve the learner? —B.L.

DESIGN YOUR OWN SERVICE MOTTO

In a few minutes you can begin designing your own motto. By revealing your core values and beliefs from a time perspective, it is possible to notice patterns that you may use to design your motto. Take a few minutes now to answer the questions posed in self-assessment 5-2 about your past, present, and future activities. Include experiences from the workplace and outside of work. Your core values do not change, whether you are at work or not. The exercise uses a *what* and *why* format to uncover what you did that was successful and why it was rewarding and satisfying for you.

When you complete this self-assessment, go back and look for patterns. Does your list include items that relate to assisting people? Have you enjoyed creating new enterprises? Does your list contain patterns that reflect certain values like persistence, dedication, or service to others? From these patterns, you can develop your own service motto.

INSIGHT TO ACTION

When I completed self-assessment 5-2, I noticed that I prefer to work alone or with only a few people to create new things. While in high school I worked in my grandfather's photography studio developing pictures. Looking back to my high school days revealed that I like to take

---

Self-Assessment 5-2.
Building a foundation for a service motto.

Directions: To uncover your philosophy and core values, consider the following questions. Write your answers in the right-hand column

Timeframe	Question	Answer
Past	What were you great at in the past (five, ten, or more years ago)?	
Past	Why did it give you satisfaction?	
Present	What do you excel at now (current calendar year)?	
Present	Why do you feel good about these activities?	
Future	What opportunities for personal growth lie ahead (within the next five years)?	
Future	Why do you anticipate that you will enjoy these activities?	

risks as exemplified by starting a photography business in high school and then a seminar business 25 years later. Both ventures posed risks to my reputation and my bank account.

Later, when I was in college, I took political science and sociology courses that provided insights on how organizations function. I attempted to apply such concepts as change management and conflict resolution to my fraternity living experience, because I enjoyed applying theoretical notions to real-life problems.

By putting these patterns together, it is perfectly clear why my service motto is "Insight to action." I enjoy helping people apply their insights in the classroom to real-life situations in the workplace. I like being a learning partner, team-teaching with other trainers, creating seminars with clients, and collaborating on this book. My service motto reflects my deepest values and core beliefs. It's who I am as a human being and as a professional trainer.—B.L.

Other interesting training service mottoes include the following:

- Discover each person's unique voice.
- Reveal the creativity in everyone.
- Uncover each person's potential.
- Create impact.
- Have fun while learning.
- Facilitate learning.
- Be flexible and open.

Dan Heck (1999), an exceptional trainer and friend, has as his motto: "I want to add value." He explains that people he teaches are hired to provide value to their organizations whether by helping to design a product or by performing a service. His role as a learning leader is to enhance their knowledge or skills so that they will add value when they return to the workplace.

LISTEN TO THE MARGIN NOTES

M idway through a training module on networking for a group of city employees, someone asked how best to remember names. There was a lot of energy around this topic, and it led to more questions about meeting people. Finally, I just stopped in the middle of my notes and we improvised on the theme of making introductions. Because the training was for city employees, someone played the role of mayor and they all practiced introducing each other. All of this was "in the margin," if you will. None of this activity had been scripted, but it was important nonetheless. "Listen to the margin notes" is my motto. What this means is that the real learning may not be written in the manual, in the book, or in the exercises. The real learning may come with the spontaneity of discussion, experience, and the nuances of the changing environment in which employees operate. —C.M.

USING YOUR SERVICE MOTTO

How should you use it? It may be used before, during, or after learning events. No matter what the timeframe, the overall purpose is always the same: Your service motto keeps you and the learners focused on what is important. It provides a context—a spacious meadow—for learning and inquiry.

Before the Event

Before a training event your service motto may be used to sell your program. When you conduct a showcase for potential clients or attendees, always begin by explaining your service motto. Use a visual logo to assist you in explaining the concept. It also helps to tell a personal story about how it was created.

E.J.'s QUESTION

I let my showcase guests know that while I was the training manager at Marshall Field's in Chicago, my manager, E.J. Milligan, asked me a question that changed my professional life. E.J. asked, "How do you know anyone ever does anything after your training classes?" That bold question hit like a bolt of lightening, and it started me on a quest: How can I focus learners on posttraining application of knowledge? The result of that quest was a commitment to move people from their own insights to take committed action back at work. My service motto reads, "Insight to action." It appears on all my manuals, stationery, and certificates.—B.L.

Besides using storytelling to explain your service motto, you should also indicate the assumptions underlying your motto. Important concepts for a service motto include the following statements:

- People already have most of the answers.
- People are able and capable of growing.
- People work well in a team learning environment.

If you are an internal training leader, you also market your programs. Your co-workers want to understand your philosophy of training, and they want to learn about the topics you are facilitating. As you chat informally with colleagues, tell them about upcoming events. Use your service motto to highlight your offerings. In published curricula and fliers, mention the way you train and the topics you are promoting. Take the same approach at company Websites and intranet locations.

Promote your special approach to training during needs analysis interviews, as well. Although the primary purpose of such interviews is to become intimate with your clients' training needs and culture, you also build trust by sharing your special approach or voice. When you are willing to share your values about training, you encourage two-way dialogue. The person you are questioning about organizational issues and training content is more likely to be open and honest when you reveal your core values. During these needs interviews, you also begin to market yourself and the topics before the training event.

During the Launch

During the critical introductory or launch phase of a training session, you should also explain your approach and methods with your service motto. Use compelling anecdotes, as you do at marketing events, during your introductory remarks. This opening phase is a critical time, because this is when you and the client agree about the methods and goals of the training session. It is during this opening period that you and the learners together create the meadow—the context or framework for inquiry—in which you play. The service motto vehicle is a natural place to begin. Assumptions about your role and the participants' role are clarified from that important jumping-off point. Ground rules may be formed. A team of learners begins to gel. Your role as servant-leader becomes clear.

During the Event

Your motto keeps you focused on your ultimate training purpose during the training. For example, if your motto involves application of learning, this fact will affect your speaking and listening throughout your training program. You can empower participants to take action through personal commitment. Consider an example: During your program, a manager says that she wants to improve her listening skills. She says she could do this by putting down everything she is doing and giving someone on her staff her full attention. You could support this goal by asking her to make a commitment to listen more attentively to her staff in the future, thereby moving her from insight to action.

Your focus on moving people from insight to action frames the way you speak and listen to participants during the class. It becomes a way of being—moving beyond mere technique. Although methods are involved, the methods reflect your motto, your purpose, and the meadow for learning that you have forged with your participants.

Another way that your motto affects your training is in the instructional design itself. Again, if your motto focused on posttraining follow-through, you might logically build in additional time to focus on commitment writing, commitment declarations, and peer-partnering for commitment support. Various formats can be used to encourage these commitment activities. These design elements all flow from your motto.

It also seems quite natural to encourage students to design their own service mottoes if the overall topic is appropriate. During customer service sessions, you can do this by first asking participants to remember a time they delivered exceptional service. Then you ask participants to write down the reason that they provided great service. You could use self-assessment 5-2 as a model for the learners.

A POIGNANT MOTTO

During *a customer service session that I led some years ago, a nurses' aide who worked in the oncology department of a community hospital told us this moving story: One evening when she came on duty, she asked a patient how she was doing. Her patient was weak from radiation treatment, so she hadn't eaten her dinner, but now she was hungry. Although the hos-*

pital kitchen was closed, the aide made the effort to go downstairs and fix the patient a fruit plate. When the aide brought the plate back for the patient, the patient offered to share the plate of fruit, saying, "This can be our love plate." The patient died two days later.

It takes a special gift to work in the oncology department. Asked why she performed this act of service, the aide responded, "Because I love my patients." Naturally, her service motto was "Love my patients." She drew a heart on a card and wrote her motto within the heart. She kept the card in sight to remind her of her commitment to serve with love.

When participants share such stories, it moves us all to do better. Hearing such tales transforms us by lifting us to higher ground. During such times we become learning partners in the profoundest sense. The leader merely provides the canvas upon which the participants paint.—B.L.

After the Event

Your service motto directs follow-up activity. When your motto aims you toward adding value, you may add value by telephoning your clients to find out how they are applying their knowledge. If your motto stresses fun, you can design a follow-up session that celebrates the progress people have made since the initial training. You may design commitment reporting into the follow-up events, if reporting naturally flows from a focus on moving people to take action.

MOTTO POWER

My service motto is "Insight to action," reflecting my commitment to focus on posttraining application of knowledge. I am often surprised by the powerful pull it exerts on my learning partners and me. Here are some examples of unexpected outcomes that resulted from encouraging workplace application:

I conducted a leadership seminar for directors at an inner-city hospital. One session focused on systems thinking. Attending were two directors of nursing, one from the emergency room and the other from surgery. Realizing that they needed to view their operations as one system rather than separate, functional departments, they declared commitments to improve the transfer of patients from each other's departments. At the next session, these two women reported lifesaving results. Because of their mutual commitment to understand each other's operations better, a gunshot patient's life had been saved. The day before the patient entered the emergency room, the two directors had met and streamlined ways to transfer patients from one department to the other. They estimated that the streamlining resulted in a 10-minute reduction in transfer time—enough time saved to enable the young shooting victim to survive!

At a session on customer service for a wholesale coffee distributor, representatives from around the country met to learn about new products and to improve service to their wholesale customers. I partnered with the training manager to design the three-day event. At the end of the program, each

customer service representative set service goal actions. Results were
reported by telephone at conference follow-up sessions two months later.
Stories began to circulate about fabulous actions that front-line staff were
initiating. One woman decided to conduct "moments of truth" sessions for
the entire Detroit office. Another saved $ 5,300 for the eastern region.
Another studied a new product manual while she covered a reception board.
Another person reported using more open-ended questions to improve com-
munication with her customers. One participant began cross-training her
staff so that all could respond to customer questions. A sampling of these
great results were published in the company magazine.—B.L.

DEVELOP YOUR OWN MOTTO

Now, you may begin designing your own motto, a philosophy of training
expressed in a clear, concise, and compelling manner. Self-assessment 5-3 will
guide you as you start the process. Your motto will provide direction, meaning,
and purpose for you as the learning leader and the learners. Use your motto as a
framework for designing, delivering, and facilitating learning.

Self-Assessment 5-3.
Service motto brainstorming activity.

Directions: To begin designing your own service motto, complete the brainstorm activity below. At the conclusion of the activity, you should have a few preliminary themes to try on for size over the next few months. Use them before, during, and after training programs. Select one that you are comfortable with and begin using it regularly. It will serve you and the people you serve.

Look back at self-assessment 5-1, the envisioning activity, and summarize in a few sentences the patterns you discovered about yourself.

Now go back over self-assessment 5-2 in which you built a foundation for a service motto. Summarize the insights or patterns you discovered about yourself when you completed that activity.

Using the insights and patterns from the above activities, it is possible to develop several service motto choices below. Remember that your service motto should be clear, concise, and compelling.

1.

2.

3.

4.

5.

SECTION 2.
CREATE A CLIMATE FOR LEARNING

6 | USE YOUR NATURAL STYLE

The first section of this book focused on you and your role. You have had an opportunity to look at your own motivations and to think about becoming intimate with clients, being a learning partner, and creating a service motto. This section looks more closely at what happens in the learning environment and, specifically, how the trainer and learners communicate.

Adult-learning expert Malcolm Knowles (1995) says that the single most important thing in helping adults learn is to create a climate conducive to learning: "It seems tragic to me that so little attention is paid to climate in traditional education." Why is climate so important? How do you, the trainer, create it? A climate is an overall atmosphere that pervades the environment. It is a prevailing set of conditions. As the learning leader, you become the thermostat, you do the fine-tuning, and you are the climate controller.

What exactly is it that you influence and control? How do you sense when a climate is conductive to learning? Knowles asks trainers to pay attention to both the physical and the psychological climates. Indeed, climate is determined by several factors: the physical space, the amount of movement, and the props and tools that are used in the environment. It can be observed in the nonverbal communication of facial expressions and body positioning of learners and trainer. It can be heard in discussions, laughter, angry comments, and in the collaborative work of activities. It can be felt in the overall atmosphere in the room, the prevailing conditions that surround the learners.

Climate-setting begins with you. Before the session, plan carefully for the climate you want by preparing yourself, your instructional materials, and your setup accordingly. During the training, you can actively influence the desired outcome through your ability to communicate. From the moment learners arrive until their departure, your communication style plays a big role in what and how adults will learn. Even in distance learning, when trainers function as discussion leaders via the Internet, the trainer sets a climate. Comments and questions still need to be addressed and encouraged or gently steered in an appropriate direction. Participants still need to feel that they are part of an open, trusting learning atmosphere. The trainer's style influences that atmosphere.

WHAT IS YOUR NATURAL STYLE?

Everyone has a natural behavioral style. As a learning leader, you may have been asked to help others determine their natural styles. You may have helped them learn how to use that style for the benefit of their work. Theorists who study behavior styles design comparative grids that contrast a variety of characteristics (for example, people versus task orientation, direct versus indirect communication style). Informative instruments, such as Myers-Briggs' Type Indicator, Carlson Learning's DISC assessment, Drake Beam Morin's I-SPEAK, and many others, can give you a sense of how you typically behave at work. They are used frequently in team building and management development, and trainers can learn from them, too.

How do you get in touch with your own natural style? First, you can analyze instances when you feel especially comfortable and effective in the learning environment. Next, you can practice specific communication techniques that let your natural style shine. You can naturalize your presentations to incorporate your strengths. Finally, you can use feedback from a variety of sources to anchor your awareness and to continue learning.

When Are You Most Comfortable and Effective?

Perhaps one of the greatest rewards for you is watching learners respond positively to your authentic presence in the room. You feel comfortable and effective; you know that you are at home in the role of trainer. Earlier in this book, you examined why you are a trainer, which is certainly a first step toward analyzing your comfort level in the role. Nevertheless, you also need to look at your effectiveness. For example, you could be very comfortable presenting information in an entertaining manner, but that approach may not always be appropriate. Conversely, you could be very comfortable facilitating a discussion and letting others be the stars, but may not always be effective.

One trainer for a company that prepares welfare recipients to get back to work in rural Nebraska builds rapport with participants as they come through the door by establishing eye contact, shaking hands, and calling them by name. You may be thinking, "Well, I do this, too. So what?" Commonly practiced warm-up activities become essential climate-building steps for such learners, who have been treated too often by society as faceless welfare cases. Trainers at this organization also discovered that they had to work to reinforce the welcoming climate. They noticed that a few negative participants were able to influence others during breaks and that the group would return in a less enthusiastic mood (Hammonds, 1999).

Now, imagine that such a welcoming manner is not part of your natural style. Perhaps you are a more reserved, analytical person who enjoys logic and pointed questions more than interpersonal actions between people. What can you do to be comfortable and effective? Is it possible to set the right climate and feel natural as well? The first step is to be aware of your behavioral style and how you communicate it to others. You can learn a great deal from written assessments; and, if you are self-aware, you can also pay attention to your experiences and to the feedback others give you. Self-assessment 6.1 will help you define your natural style.

Self-Assessment 6-1.
What is your natural style?

Directions: Here are some words that describe behavioral characteristics. Circle the ones that apply to you at work or write in your own ideas.

humble	risk taker	charming	patient	analytical
generous	persuasive	bold	diplomatic	kind
forceful	impulsive	predictable	accurate	competitive
sociable	deliberate	talkative	introspective	adventurous
humorous	persistent	cooperative	dependable	organized
argumentative	gracious	curious	unconventional	conventional
approachable	shy	follower	leader	initiator
creative	trusting	questioning	daring	supportive
assertive	listening	challenging	dogmatic	other_____

Complete these sentences:

My co-workers have described me as . . .

My superiors or clients have described me as . . .

My learners have described me as . . .

If you are aware of your commonly practiced behaviors, the next step is to keep your behavior aligned with the objectives of your job. If you are a conscientious, task-oriented person, who, as a trainer, needs to encourage groups to feel welcome, you can set yourself up for success by thinking ahead. You can plan for the climate you want and provide learners with a natural opportunity to get to know you by

- rehearsing your opening comments
- setting your room in advance so that you can stand at the door without worry
- keeping ready a couple of nonthreatening topics to open conversation, for example, a local sports team or some current event.

Now, imagine that you are a trainer with a natural, outgoing personality who bubbles with energy and natural charm. You are in the same position of making welfare recipients feel welcome. How can you be both comfortable and effective in the role? "Easy!" you may say, "I love helping people feel at ease. It's my forte." A person with your style, however, needs to be aware that these learners may initially mistrust someone with a great deal of energy and charm; you may need to tone down your enthusiasm to a quiet approachability. Paradoxically, your strength becomes your weakness. Certainly, you do not want to assume that everyone is as comfortable as you are about sharing information with others. In fact, trainers with this bubbly style do well at the beginning of a session but often have difficulty maintaining the energy throughout. They may take the lead once too often, cease listening, and, finally, their learners stop contributing altogether.

How Can You Let Your Natural Style Shine?

Suzanne Meyering, a career coach with a background in sociology, has spent many hours studying how to help her clients bring their natural styles to work. When asked what would help trainers be more authentic, she suggested that they consider what deepens and moves the learning forward. Because trainers are seen as experts, as people who add value, they may feel an exaggerated need to justify themselves, when all their audiences really want is for them to be real. "The ego trap is an easy trap," Meyering (1999) adds. "People don't trust you if they feel that you're holding back the truth. You act in a way so that people don't know something, but what you're hiding is what people notice."

BEING NATURAL: LESSONS LEARNED

Early in my training career, my boss was observing as I initiated a new class for supervisors. I was very nervous. The room was set up in a U-shaped format. I was sitting at the head of the U on a swivel chair. At the first break, the manager noted that I jumped up and down off that chair 15 times during the first 10 minutes! I was using up my nervous energy in a very distracting fashion. Certainly my nervousness did not enhance my training effectiveness.

Consider the times in the past when you were most comfortably effective as a trainer. What did you do? How did the group respond? How did the climate look, sound, and feel? How can you recapture that climate for future training events? Over the years, I learned to channel my energy by staying centered in one spot during opening remarks and projecting my voice. What looks easy and natural often takes some time to practice and realize.—B.L.

The blend of who you are and what learners need is a delicate balance. Often in formal education, learners are conditioned to learn without a personal connection to the instructor; it is sometimes hard to find good models for this skill. Moreover, personal connection may entail taking risks. You become more transparent. Sometimes letting your natural style shine means letting your weaknesses shine, too. It means being honest with participants, perhaps saying things such as, "This is a difficult topic for me, too. I know there are a lot of strong feelings about it." It might mean taking more time to rehearse how you will present topics that are difficult for you. It might mean asking co-workers to provide inside information beforehand so that you will achieve the comfort level you want with the group.

A BEGINNING PRESENTER'S JITTERS

I was asked to speak on listening to a local association of business and professional women. As I delivered the introduction, I glanced up to see the owner of the small firm I worked for at the time pacing across the back of the room, smoking a cigarette. Seeing the boss's nervousness just added *fuel to my own jitters, and I would have given anything at that point for some experience—any experience—in public speaking. Did these people think me a fraud who really didn't know a thing about listening? I even began to question my own credentials. Somehow, I fumbled my way through, but I can't imagine that any semblance of my real self came through in that presentation.*

Over time, I've come to trust my natural style—my sense of humor, good sportsmanship, and anger when people don't play fair. Although I enjoy spontaneous sharing of ideas, I secretly worry about how such digressions will affect the schedule; you see, at heart, I am task-oriented and like things to go as planned.

I've learned to live by my service mottoes, "Listen to the margin notes," and "Focus on them." These overriding themes help maintain the balance between my natural style and the leadership style that will best serve the learners. I don't always succeed; no trainer can exactly predict the human element.—C.M.

With experience, most trainers can bring more of their authentic selves to their message. O'Neill (1996) cautions new trainers not to let the method of delivery—the multimedia equipment, the games, or the role plays—overshadow the content. She also advises trainers avoid letting their personalities outshine the goals of the training. Trainers are there to provide clear content and a learning experience.

HOW CAN YOU NATURALIZE YOUR PRESENTATIONS?

Most training delivery continues to be the presentation of material by an instructor in a classroom. Your presentation style, therefore, plays a large role in setting the climate and influencing how adults learn. Whether you are briefly introducing a topic or delivering a hefty technical lecture, your job is to present in a manner that is adaptable to the needs of the group. This adaptability is important for effective presentations; by being flexible, you can find a style that keeps you and the learners comfortable. To naturalize your presentations is to be your natural self with a spacious meadow for flexibility.

Danielle Kennedy, a motivational speaker and successful real estate saleswoman, reinforces the importance of being natural in every step of the sale, from the cold call to the close. Recalling her nervousness as a new salesperson, she credits her husband as a staunch supporter who told her to ". . . just be your natural self" (Kennedy, 1984). She started her career that way, asking questions and applying different approaches for different types of customers. As she grew in experience, she continued to learn that ". . . the natural salesperson dances to the beat of the customer." Trainers can do that too, especially when they present.

How can you make your delivery more natural? How can you learn to dance to the beat of your customers? It begins with preparation. How comfortable you are in front of a group depends on how much work you do up front. Perhaps you have had the opportunity to hear an especially effective professional speaker. Professional speakers are often praised for their ability to make presenting look easy. When they are asked how they do it, their response is typically, "Practice, practice, practice." Natural communicators know that they have prepared to be the best that they can be at that moment with the group. You, too, can be a natural communicator through practice. Your practice should encompass three essential elements: attention to what you are saying, how you are saying it, and why you are saying it. The most significant element is why.

Why Are You There?

Aristotle, the Greek philosopher and scholar of persuasion, wrote in 2300 B.C. that of the three components of a presentation—the talk, the audience, and the speaker—the audience was by far the most important (Cooper, 1932). Any presentation designed for the audience has a strong likelihood of succeeding. If you have become truly intimate with your client, you are ready to give a natural presentation. You are clear about why you are there.

Tied to your reason for being is your credibility as a presenter. Conger (1998a) acknowledges, "We build credibility around two factors: expertise and relationships." He advises that you consider your strengths in both dimensions and focus your presentation planning on the weaker dimension. For example, if you are preparing to present to an audience that perceives your expertise but has no relationship with you, consider doing some networking before the session to learn something about the people who will be in the room. In contrast, if your relationship is strong but your perceived expertise is weak, you may want to build documentation, testimonials, interviews, or success stories to build your credibility.

PERCEPTIONS COUNT

I was asked to present two short communication-skill sessions for an international sales meeting of a global manufacturer. Because I was referred for the job, my perceived expertise was strong, however, I had no relationship with the organization at all. My responsibility was to build that relationship through talking with the vice president of sales and the HR director on the telephone. They had already agreed to use my services, but they really didn't know me. We had several conversations, and it took a little longer than usual to tailor the program, but it was necessary to earn their trust. Together, we worked to ensure that the tone of the presentation was appropriate. What I learned from those conversations was that this meeting was a risk; it was the first of its kind and it was much needed to unify the sales force. The information had to be geared to intelligent, highly motivated individuals who were also questioning why their time was to be spent in this meeting. Developing a relationship with the vice president of sales helped me position myself with the group.

The opposite situation arose later that same week. I was asked to do a similar program for a long-time client who requested a motivational session for a customer-service staff retreat. She was planning the session with the vice president of operations, someone with whom I was unacquainted. I was entering the presentation with strong relationship power with her, but I had none with him. I needed to build my perceived expertise with both of them. The topic was a new one, and the vice president of operations had

never seen my programs. We met to plan the training, and I spent a consid-
erable amount of time suggesting a variety of approaches based on past
programs. In essence, I was building my perceived expertise with examples
of past successes.—C.M.

So, the first practice step is being clear about why you are there. Once you eliminate any doubts; you have the freedom to be yourself. If you feel comfortable in your own credibility, if you are clear about your purpose, and if you have built the relationship to the best of your ability, you have set yourself up for success as a natural.

What Are You Saying?

Being clear about why you are there is only the pencil sketch behind what will eventually become your true colors as a presenter. Your words are also important; they make your presentation uniquely yours. What you say in the first hour or so of a training presentation is important. During this time, you are creating a first impression that will be difficult to change. There are three essential pieces to making the first part of your presentation effective:

- Warm up participants to you.
- Warm up participants to each other.
- Warm up participants to the topic.

These pieces work together much like the parts of an Oreo cookie; it takes all three pieces to create the unique flavor that you want. Practice the opening of every presentation you do so that all three parts are included.

Warm Up Participants to You. Aristotle wrote, "The character of the speaker is one of the most potent of all the means to persuasion" (Cooper, 1932). How do you reveal your character? Character is revealed by how you share your beliefs and the language that you use to do it. It is revealed in your emotional response to issues and in your intellectual response to shared inquiry. Aristotle wrote a lot about ethos. Ethos can be seen as competence, trustworthiness, and dynamism.

What exactly are these qualities? If you are competent, you are trained, qualified, skilled, and informed. A trustworthy person is kind, congenial, friendly, forgiving, and hospitable. A dynamic presenter has an ability to be emphatic, bold, forceful, and energetic. Robbins (1990) asked learners about specific trainer behaviors that make learning a positive experience. She learned that positive learning experiences were associated with trainers who were kind, fair, knowledgeable, "human," and who offered humor and encouragement. Negative learning experiences were associated with trainers who were judgmental, dogmatic, insensitive, disorganized, and lacking knowledge.

Through their words, trainers can achieve credibility by incorporating references to their research, to the situation and the audience, and to their own backgrounds. Even in opening remarks, trainers can tie their research into an example to which the group can relate. For instance, if you are leading a workshop on effective employee orientations, you could say, "Good morning. I would like you to think of me for a moment as Jane Newcomer, a new person in your department.

I am one of 80,000 other Americans for whom today is the first day on the job. Overnight I have gone from being a respected member of one group to an utterly unknown quantity—a rookie—in another. It cost you about $8,000 to hire me, but I will probably be gone in three years." This type of opening establishes not only that you did your statistical homework but also that you can take a creative approach to the topic.

Another method of using words effectively is borrowed from the art of persuasion; it is called the assimilation effect. It refers to an audience's tendency to believe a presenter more strongly whom they consider to be like them. Politicians have applied this effect to their benefit for years. Trainers can also use it, so long as it is an attempt to build an honest relationship. For example, if you have performed the same job as your learners, you can mention it. Alternatively, you can establish that you, too, are a learner and mention some classes that you are taking.

The more naturally you can bring your own background into the learning, the better you can establish ethos. You can build upon any common work experiences. For example, one trainer, when working with any type of telephone professional, always mentions the eight years she spent on the telephone making 50 cold calls a day for a sales training firm. Trainers from the New York office of one bank send brief biographies with a greeting letter and preliminary materials when they are working with other branches and locations. Outside consultants can easily provide a brief biographical sketch before the training via email or in the pre-work materials. People like to relate to others' life experiences.

If you have established your credibility by incorporating references to your research, your background, and your related experiences, you have taken a first step to warming them up to you.

Warm Up Participants to Each Other. The second part of establishing a warm, open climate is to use your natural style to get participants talking to each other. Too often, trainers skip this essential ingredient in climate setting. Have you ever been to a workshop where this was not done? Did you spend time wondering about the others who were there and what they thought?

The type of icebreaker you use should fit the topic, the audience, and your own style. Some ideas that often work well are partner introductions and sharing of expectations and challenges. There are many creative ways to warm up participants, and you can select among them. Some trainers ask people to meet someone else in the room and then introduce themselves as that person. Others ask participants to list 10 things they excel at or to reveal details that very few people know about them.

How do participant warm-ups allow you to be natural? They immediately bring a comfort level to the room, they allow everyone to interact more naturally, they dispel fears, and they set the tone for what is to come. They allow you to present with ease and comfort. As you plan your warm-ups, consider the following:

- Do they need to know each others' names?
- Will there be any ill feelings about each other?
- Will there be hesitancies to speak out?
- Are they strangers or frequent co-workers?

- Do they see each other every day?
- Are they new or long-time employees?

You can often establish a comfortable climate with strangers more easily than with frequent co-workers. With strangers, there are no preconceived opinions about each other to overcome. Frequent co-workers also deserve your attention to make them feel comfortable. A good warm-up can often dispel unspoken issues or tensions.

Warm Up Participants to the Topic. You might find yourself leading learners who feel less-than-positive about the topic. Perhaps it is a class required for promotion or credit; perhaps it deals with a controversial topic such as sexual harassment, or maybe the learners think they already know the topic, for example, communication skills. Your style as a presenter frames their perception of the topic. Of course, well-written introductory material helps, but how it is delivered—the tone and the energy that you share—will influence their perceptions.

Imagine that the employee orientation training that you are leading does not typically interest learners. One way to warm them to the topic is by asking them about their own orientation experiences. Frequently, people have unbelievable, hilarious stories about their first days on a job. Perhaps one person arrived at the workplace without anyone knowing who they were, or maybe someone was sent to an empty desk in a shabby corner. Getting experiences like these out in the open sets the stage for the topic. Some trainers immediately address the unpopularity of the topic and then ask learners why that topic may possibly benefit them. Team building, for example, is a topic that, depending on the company's culture, can receive negative reactions. In such a case, the trainer could ask learners why a team might be more beneficial than an individual. Often learners have not really thought about it. In this scenario, learners can come up with their own reasons.

If you pay attention to the three-part warm-up, you will be able to communicate naturally. Trainers who start cold are setting themselves up with unresponsive learners; they make it harder to share their style. Assess your natural warm-up style with self-assessment 6-2.

Of course, it is important to practice the words you will say after the warm-up period is over. A huge trainer manual can be daunting. You may think, "How can I get through all of this and sound natural?" If you divide the trainer notes into sections, highlighting key points, and making notes in the margin to yourself, you can prepare to look and sound more familiar with the text. Practice aloud. As is true for professional speakers, you, too, will benefit from practice. Your eyes will become accustomed to where words are on the page; you can even practice repeating difficult definitions and explanations. When you have presented the same program repeatedly, it will be easier to incorporate your own words into the prepared content.

How Are You Saying It?
You have considered why you are there and what you are saying, especially in the first hour or so of the training session. You are beginning to color your natural style more fully. Now you need to consider how you are delivering the information you

---

Self-Assessment 6-2.
What is your warm-up style?

Directions: Keeping in mind when you feel both comfortable and effective, consider the first hour or so of your training presentations and answer the following questions.

What have you done to help the group warm up to you? What could you do that you have not done before?

What have you used as warm-up methods? What are some additional ways you can comfortably ask participants to warm up to each other?

With which methods are you comfortable warming up the group to the topic?

---

have planned so carefully. Delivery tools fall into two basic categories: verbal and nonverbal. Verbal delivery tools are your voice tone, pitch, speed, and volume. They include paralinguistics (body language of the voice) such as accent, pause rate, and use of the language. Nonverbal delivery tools consist of body and face gestures, including stance and movement, nodding, and facial expression. There are three tips to remember as you consider how to use your tools of delivery:

- Adjust to the situation.
- Be fresh.
- Be emotionally compelling.

First, adjust to the situation. For example, imagine that you have planned a particularly dynamic energetic opening, only to learn moments before your session that the group faced a downsizing that morning. How might you use your delivery tools to adjust to this situation? You will want to tone down enthusiasm and be serious with equally serious people, but you will want to maintain vocal and body energy to keep them engaged and help them face the future. You will want to communicate your natural empathy to their situation.

As a trainer, your responsibility is to the needs of the group and the needs of the organization. Experienced trainers find ways to balance the two by selecting the right tools to help them convey the message they want. Establishing eye contact with individuals establishes rapport; planned movements and use of pauses shows confidence; pleasant and approachable facial expressions convey caring. The larger the group, the bigger the expressions need to be. With a small, seminar-style group, you may want to sit with them frequently and lower your volume and gesture to fit their size.

Second, be fresh. Avoid making stale presentations. A common challenge that trainers face is keeping material fresh in the face of repetition. You may be in charge of the new employee orientation, presenting the same information every two weeks. According to O'Neill (1996), "If you encourage responsiveness . . . you guarantee that each session will have its own signature character." Signature character is an interesting way to approach training that you repeat often. Every class indeed has its own character.

Approach each training session with renewed energy. The delightful thing about the training profession is what is unknown, that is, how each group of learners will behave. You will have the opportunity to answer new questions and to answer old questions in new ways. People will tell their own stories, and you will have an opportunity to relate to them in new ways. Keep your delivery fresh with what actors call the illusion of the first time. Your learners must feel as if you have never delivered the material before. Do not be too quick to make assumptions about how they will respond.

Third, be emotionally compelling. Natural trainers are able to get beyond the facts to the stories that color the facts. You have already learned how to use storytelling to become intimate with the client. Storytelling is also a powerful delivery tool to encourage emotional involvement with the topic. For example, if you are training a group of technical people in information technology about how to provide better customer service, you can tell the organization's service success stories to illustrate concepts. Riskier, yet very effective, is the sharing of your own stories, especially when you have learned through failure in some way.

MELLOWING MEL

When working with new trainers, I always tell stories about training challenges. For example, I often relay stories about difficult participants I've encountered. One such story that I tell is about Mel, an insurance industry claims officer who would fold his arms and look defensive every time I mentioned anything having to do with homework or action planning. Finally, I asked him if he was bothered or troubled in some way. He said, "I like training better when we just show up, read the book, and go home." Usually this story evokes some laughter, certainly empathy, from the partic-

*ipants. We continue by discussing just what you should do with such defen-
sive behavior in a training session. In Mel's case, we talked one-on-one
after the class about his busy schedule and lack of time to complete extra
work. I emphasized how much more meaningful the outcome of the two
days in class would be if he took the time now to do some work. He never
did agree totally, but he did arrive the next day with a brief summary and
referred to it in discussion.—C.M.*

Storytelling is only one tool for adding emotion to your training. Storytelling
is also a skill; it involves using all of your delivery tools—face, body, and voice—
to maximum advantage. It is not easy, but the natural presenter can practice using
these tools to achieve a natural style.

To be emotionally compelling is to be alert to the nuances in the atmosphere
of the session, whether you are riding the excitement of the group or being fully
attentive to the fears or pain you sense in the group. The emotionally compelling
presenter is not afraid to say, "You were absolutely wonderful today. You really
attacked that bug in the software." The emotionally compelling presenter can also
say, " I am saddened that the rate of change is so slow, and, like you, I look forward to what's ahead." You are human when you make comments such as these.
You are your natural self.

HOW CAN YOU USE FEEDBACK TO BUILD AUTHENTICITY?

Trainers receive much feedback. Feedback is inherent in your role from beginning
to end, especially feedback on your presentation style, which is most visible to
most people. Feedback is an important tool for self-awareness and for social com-
parison. By comparing yourself to others who fill similar roles, you gain knowledge
about yourself and your behavior. Because people tend to have judging natures,
most people are prone to give feedback with ease. Asking for feedback, however, is
more difficult. An ability to ask for feedback is a mark of healthy maturity. Sorting
out which feedback is most meaningful is a continual learning process.

RUDY'S FEEDBACK REMEMBERED

I *was about to give an important presentation to all of the vice presidents
at Marshall Field's regarding the next year's training initiative. Before the
talk, the president, Rudy Hirsch, observed, "What's wrong, Lyerly? You look
nervous today." I replied that I was. His next remarks forever changed me:
"Why waste your time being nervous. Don't you know that 50 percent of
these people think you're a jerk anyway? Hey, 75 percent think I'm a jerk!"
After the initial blow of the statement subsided, I realized that Rudy was
telling me that no matter how great my presentation was, some people
weren't going to like it, so I might as well forget about trying to please
everyone. Rudy's principle can certainly help you maintain your sanity.
Unless you are coaching one-on-one, you are most likely presenting information to a group with diverse opinions and ideas.—B.L.*

Robin Sheerer (1999), a career coach, interviewed hundreds of people for her recent book. She observes, "All of us have negative behaviors. We probably developed them as defenses when we were children. They may have been appropriate at that time, but as adults we are hindered when people around us are afraid to give us feedback." Sheerer cautions that, though we are skilled at our defensive behaviors, we are often unaware of how they affect others. Perhaps unknowingly, we train our friends and family members not to give us uncomfortable feedback, and finally, they stop.

DO I DO THAT?

I once piloted a three-day program for new supervisors and had a great deal of information to remember. My client observed each day from the back of the room, critiquing both my content and training style. During the break after one particularly stressful unit, the client told me, with an expression of mild distaste, that I had repeated something three times, each time only slightly differently. I felt defensive but thanked him for his observation. Later, when I cooled down, I realized that what he said was true: When nervous, I tend to repeat or emphasize information needlessly, perhaps grasping for a segue to the next idea. So, as difficult as it was for me to hear that feedback, it was truthful and I learned from it. I work hard not to repeat information needlessly, especially when I feel stressed.—C.M.

Feedback is a gift because it gives you an opportunity to learn about yourself and to change your behavior. Feedback can also be debilitating if given without thought. It is important to consider feedback as one more way to help you grow professionally. Positive feedback, if given with sincerity, should be accepted with sincerity. Many trainers find it difficult to accept compliments on their hard work. Take them; you earned them, and thank the giver.

When possible, try to find objective forms of feedback to help you grow. Mentors are usually astute at delivering careful feedback; audiotape and videotape do not lie. Even strangers you may meet in professional-development classes can be effective, unbiased givers of feedback. You can search out other effective feedback tools, too. The right amount of feedback will help you grow into your natural presentation style.

SETTING THE CLIMATE WITH YOUR NATURAL STYLE

When you are comfortable with yourself and your reason for being there, then that ease will transfer to the learning climate. Creating an effective learning climate is the ultimate goal for the skilled learning leader in the classroom. When you can focus on the participants rather than yourself, your natural style will shine through. From how you plan your opening words to how you receive the final feedback, you affect how learners learn. It is worth taking a close look at your style strengths and challenges. It is a delicate balance of credibility with approachability. To help you achieve this delicate balance, assess your style frequently (self-assessment 6-3).

Self-Assessment 6-3.
How can I apply my natural style?

Directions: List six characteristics that you know to be your natural style as a trainer.

1.

2.

3.

4.

5.

6.

How does your natural style add value to the work that you do with adult learners? Complete this sentence: I bring value because I am able to . . .

1.

2.

3.

How does your natural style keep you from being as effective as you might like to be? Complete this sentence: I am challenged by and need to be alert to . . .

1.

2.

3.

7 | LISTEN TO LEARN

American dramatist Wilson Mizner once wrote, "A good listener is not only popular everywhere, but after a while he or she knows something" (Prochnow, 1952). Everyone admires a good listener, but good listening is more than just good etiquette. Good listeners may indeed be well mannered, but, more importantly, they are smart. They are smart because they are constantly learning. They are open to impromptu learning. They are also receptive to the idea that listening is hard work, that it is a skill and a discipline.

Trainers who can listen actively are the most effective learning leaders. Aubrey and Cohen (1995) quote a training professional: "Learning is the ongoing practice of what you do; it's not something you can package neatly and transfer to another person." In this chapter, you will examine listening as part of that ongoing learning practice. It is impossible to package listening neatly, because it is a skill that relies on your ability to adapt constantly—mentally, physically, and verbally—to the nuances of the learner's situation. To help you adapt, you will analyze the barriers to listening that may be affecting you and select among specific techniques to help overcome them. You will also learn how to listen in difficult situations. Finally, you will apply listening skills to energize and adapt to the nuances of the group. Listening to learn is indeed a journey, and you can make margin notes all along the way.

When should you make margin notes? The right time is anytime during your training sessions. No seminar or coaching session is straightforward, perfectly choreographed, and right on schedule. Your wisdom is tied directly to your ability to listen to what the learners are saying. Hear and make notes about what is happening at the margins. Aubrey and Cohen (1995) have seen this spontaneity in their study of workplace wisdom: "The most profound learning usually unfolds through unplanned, unscripted, and untidy episodes." Learning is never perfect and never ends, so it provides the ultimate opportunity for listening well.

WHAT MAKES LISTENING DIFFICULT?

Naturally, you are built to be able to listen well: You have ears, eyes, and a sense of inquiry. Nevertheless, these senses also allow in distractions, a variety of stimuli that can then become barriers to effective listening. These barriers can be grouped into three types: physical, intellectual, and emotional.

Physical barriers are those caused by the environment and your own physical health. Is the room small, windowless, and colorless? Is it too noisy? Are there distractions surrounding the place where learning should be occurring? Physically, are you in good form? Are you calm and rested, or are you tired and hungry? Physical barriers are a common cause of ineffective listening.

Intellectual barriers are those that affect your ability to comprehend. They may come in the form of clichés or archaic, unfamiliar words. Foreign phrases, technical jargon, oversimplified language, even a beautifully delivered, poetic phrase—all can cause intellectual stops. A learner who overuses "technobabble" can be just as difficult to listen to as someone who speaks in an unfamiliar language.

Emotional barriers can erupt as reactions to certain types of people or messages. Are you threatened by the topic at hand? Do you disagree with it strongly? Do you feel antagonistic toward the learner? Do you have a personal bias toward the learner? Do you have a personal bias toward one particular training method that has proven successful repeatedly? Success presents a paradox: The more experience or degrees people have and the more renown they achieve in their field, the less open they become to other ideas. This paradox can present emotional barriers to listening.

In addition to these three types of barriers, another built-in listening barrier exists. Most people are able to think faster than others talk; their minds race ahead of the conversation. This extra thought time results in bad listening habits; between words and sentences, you have time to formulate what you will say next, to manufacture arguments, and to daydream. Using thought time effectively is a real discipline. Consider the words of Charles Rossotti (1999), commissioner of the Internal Revenue Service, "People seem to think that they're being most productive when they're accomplishing a bunch of tasks. But I've found that the best use of my time at the IRS is to listen."

The first step to overcoming listening barriers is to identify them. Self-assessment 7-1 can help you become aware of physical, intellectual, emotional, and thought-speech barriers to good listening.

HOW CAN YOU LISTEN ACTIVELY?

Writer Gertrude Stein once said, "Everyone, when they are young, has a little bit of genius. That is, they really do listen. Then they grow a little older and many of them get tired and listen less and less" (Adler, 1983). Does this describe you? Does this describe you on a day when you are feeling burnt out? Perhaps you heard a message but chose not to listen? How about programs that you facilitate repeatedly? Do you get tired and listen less and less?

Listening is more than just hearing, which is a physical process. Hearing is a special sense by which the brain processes sound waves. It is a passive process. Most people are born with an ability to hear unless they are hearing-disabled at birth. Listening is an active process. Listening is a learned behavior. It involves attaching meaning to the sound. The process of sending and receiving messages is perhaps the most difficult role in the communication model. Some people think the sender has the most responsibility for clear messages. Actually, the receiver

Self-Assessment 7-1.
Your listening barriers.

Directions: Awareness of barriers is the first step toward better listening. Below are some categories of listening barriers. Circle the ones that affect you most frequently in learning environments (as a trainer or coach). Add any that you are aware of that are not listed. Then, look at your responses. Do your personal barriers appear in all categories? Are they concentrated in one? Determine areas where you can work to become a better listener.

Physical Barriers	Intellectual Barriers	Emotional Barriers	Thought-Speech Time Difference
Noise	Unfamiliar content	No incentive to listen	Formulating next words
Visual distractions	Unfamiliar jargon, word usage	Defensive reaction to what is said	Daydreaming
Room climate	Learner's language or accent	Personal problems unrelated to topic or learner	Planning defense or argument
Fatigue	Incorrect message	Bias toward the topic	Thinking too far ahead
Health problems	Inability to apply information	Bias toward the learner, either positive or negative	Other:
Pain or discomfort	Inability to synthesize information	Lack of motivation	
Hearing loss	Trying to do two things at once	Other:	
Other:	Other:		

does, because the receiver has to interpret and respond. Listening is far more tiring than talking.

"Active listening" is a term that was first used by psychologist Carl Rogers (1961) to refer to the work and activity involved in the listening process. Rogers encouraged the listener to work along with the speaker to help the speaker communicate. The listener takes responsibility for the success of the communication. Here are a couple of questions to ask yourself: How do you know when someone is really listening to you? How do you know when you are really listening to someone? Active listening requires mental, physical, and verbal effort.

The first step to listening actively is called attending. Attending keeps you in the moment; it focuses on the immediate. It is akin to driving your car on a snowy day. All the turns and stops that normally take very little effort now take all your concentration. Attending to a message means that:

- Mentally, you clear your mind of distractions, observe the other's nonverbal cues, make mental summaries of what has been said, and fight any defensive response that may arise.
- Physically, you maintain eye contact, keep your body posture alert, including a slight leaning-in, keep open, uncrossed arms and legs, and face the learner squarely. You work to avoid distracting behaviors, such as doodling, bouncing a pen, fiddling with jewelry, drumming fingers, eating, adjusting your hair, or looking away frequently.
- Vocally, you use brief confirming responses, such as, "I see," "I understand," "Uh-huh," "Oh?" "Yes," "Hmmm."

Attending skills encourage you to concentrate and respond in a neutral manner. The learner can sense your attending skills and will respond favorably. Attending skills encourage an open communication climate. As veteran broadcaster and listener Hugh Downs said in a recent newspaper interview, "My technique has always been to make the person feel as at home as possible. I don't believe in scalpel interviews. Listening is the first fundamental" (Mackay, 1999). Obviously, it is listening that has allowed Hugh Downs to so successfully create the open climate of his interviews.

Once you have established that you are attending, you may wish to paraphrase or restate what the learner has said. This means simply putting his or her information in your own words. You may say something like, "Jane, you've said that in your experience, internal customer service could use some improvement in your area. Is that correct?" When restating, it is important to avoid parroting or mimicking the other's words exactly. It is also important not to begin every restatement with the same phrase, such as, "What I hear you saying is . . ." which can be annoying. When misused, paraphrasing or restatement can actually block effective communication.

When used correctly, however, restatement has additional benefits. For one, restating information is an excellent way to maintain focus. When you encourage someone to verify what you have heard, you are asking for their agreement. Restating information also saves time. If your learners are not convinced that you understand what they are saying to you, they will keep repeating the same thing. A good restatement takes care of that.

Related to restating or paraphrasing is a listening skill called perception checking. When learners make statements, they include both feelings and facts. A perception check acknowledges that you are attempting to understand feelings. For example, if Joe says, "I don't understand why the managers aren't here," an answer such as, "They weren't able to come," responds only to the facts. This may be a perfectly suitable response unless Joe says it with anger. In that case, a possible perception check might be, "It sounds like you feel strongly about this, Joe." A perception check can also allow you to gauge the group's feelings: "I sense that this is a stressful issue for you. Am I right?"

Mary Samusevich (1999), a veteran training and development employee with Nicor Gas, shares a lesson that she learned about listening early in her career: "A young supervisor brought up a difficult situation that he had faced and how he had handled an issue with a problem employee. I indicated that I thought he handled the situation incorrectly. This was a very bad mistake! That comment made him a nonparticipant. In hindsight, I believe I was not listening. I was anxious to speak and to give my opinion. He was looking for help and encouragement. Instead, I diminished his self-esteem." Mary knows now that she could have asked others in the room how they would have handled it, suggested that she and the supervisor talk at break, or asked *how* and *what* questions to encourage him to see it differently. She could have checked her perception first.

In the next chapter, you will learn how to ask great questions, but you cannot ask great questions without listening first. You have to know something about the learner. You have to prepare in advance. You can listen to learn by attending, restating, and perception checking. Then you can ask even greater questions that will probe, clarify, challenge, and explore.

HOW CAN YOU LISTEN IN DIFFICULT SITUATIONS?

As a trainer, you have probably had to practice staying calm under fire in the learning environment. Participant anger, disappointment, and distrust are often communicated by venting. Venting is just what it says—letting air out. It is how participants release the feelings they are experiencing through body language, angry words, and a loud, angry tone of voice. Active listening helps you stay calm; it helps you listen with the intent to move forward. To listen effectively to harsh comments or difficult participants, you need to know how to focus on the present and depersonalize issues.

Tony Malloy, an experienced training and organizational development professional, shares his approach, "I have learned that even with my best preparation and delivery, some participants are not going to show interest or at worse become disruptive during the training presentation. The best thing to do is to acknowledge that it is their perspective. This is not anything personally against me. I do not spend as much time now as in the past trying to convert disruptive people. My focus is more on helping to retain a productive program that allows the participants to be fully involved." He adds, "It's amazing how much a client, participant, or co-worker can teach me about improving my communication and listening skills. Humility is something that I have found comes with experience. It is wise to let other people see a genuine, open-minded training professional" (Malloy, 1999).

Customer service author Clay Carr (1990) writes, "All solutions lie in the present or future. No solutions lie in the past." Angry participants tend to focus on the past, on "what was done to them." Listen for how to bring the problem to the present. For example, imagine a learner says, "We always talk about this stuff and nothing ever changes." To stay focused on the present, you could say, "I'm sorry you feel that way. What is it about today's ideas that you believe won't work?"

As you listen, use your extra thought time to depersonalize the issue instead of getting defensive. Repeat to yourself, "This isn't personal." Give an active listener's response to reassure the participant that you listened and are trying to understand: "I understand your concern, and I am sorry." This could also be called the control-your-own-defensiveness step. Whether you have to count to 10 or bite your tongue, do not react defensively. Take the learner's viewpoint professionally, not personally.

HOW CAN LISTENING HELP YOU ENERGIZE A GROUP?

As a trainer, you often listen to people who are in groups. There is a continuous pattern of activity and energy—a certain dynamic—that occurs when people learn in groups. Effective trainers are able to listen to this interpersonal underworld of the group and sense its patterns and nuances. They are able to make mental and written margin notes. They are able to use their perception of the group to select energizing ideas and activities that will move the learning forward. Those activities typically involve action, reaction, and traction for enhanced recall, retention, and application.

Perception is the first step. Perception is an honest awareness of what is going on among group members. For example, they may look bored, angry, or anxious to talk. You may see confused looks, sidelong glances, or raised eyebrows. You may hear whispering or giggles. A trainer's mental margin notes begin here. It is important to first acknowledge these behaviors mentally and then decide what to do about them. The mistake that many trainers make is not acknowledging the nonverbal and verbal behaviors of the group.

Consultant and trainer Eric Baron (1995) did some soul-searching about training after attending a tennis camp. When he was assigned to a practice group that he did not relate to, he realized that trainers need to be proactive about managing classroom groups. Are members of the small groups allowed to switch groups? Do they mix and mingle enough? Does the trainer sense any tension? When people are left out, is the group encouraged to include them? When someone is taking over, is it suggested that he or she allow others to contribute? Trainer perception is an important first step to knowing if a group needs a change.

Howard Prager, director of corporate leadership programs at the Lake Forest Graduate School of Management, defines real listening as "listening astutely with all of your senses—seeing the nonverbal and hearing what's being said underneath." He adds, "Listening happens not only when working with the client but also when working on the client." He believes that indirect processing and checking intuition is as meaningful a listening skill as the face-to-face interaction that occurs in planning or conducting a learning initiative (Prager, 1999).

You can learn to process and check perceptions continually in a learning environment. Today's learners provide you with ample opportunity. For example, you may be facing several generations in one group. Research on motivation across age groups shows that younger learners often want to manipulate data, fast-forwarding past things they do not want to hear. Baby boomers and "pre-boomers" appreciate the personal aspect of classroom learning (Kennedy, 1999). After perception checking, you select methods to move the learning forward and keep the group energized. These methods involve action, reaction, and traction.

Using action means encouraging the group to stand up, move, and mingle. For example, you could invite the participants to talk with others at another table and discuss how they got their names or how they arrived at their jobs. Here are some other action ideas you may wish to try:

- Ask everyone to come up and put something on a flipchart.
- Ask the groups to assemble at flipcharts to work together to create a graphic.
- Ask one group to stand and join another.
- Ask group members to stand up to indicate their responses: "Stand up if you have ever encountered a difficult customer first thing in the morning."

Another way to energize a group is to ask for reaction. Involvement is usually an effective learning technique. Chris Haid, regional training director for Wendy's International, says that the importance of seeking to understand the other is the most valuable lesson he has learned in more than 20 years of working with learners in the fast-food industry. He feels that seeking to understand is anchored in what he calls "competency in the art of the question." Haid (2000) believes that questions " . . . keep the focus on the other person, signaling the caring and trust necessary for meaningful partnering." Questions are indeed important in the communication process. To ask effective questions, you need to listen. To encourage an honest reaction from learners, you can ask questions such as these:

- What concerns do you have?
- How is everyone doing?
- What questions do you have?
- How does this fit in with your work?
- How do you feel about this?
- What is going on in your minds at this moment?

Another method to check in with learners is using *I*-statements that are part of the skill of perception-checking. *I* statements help communicate the trainer's ownership of the feeling expressed; for example:

- I sense that people are tired.
- I would like to check in with you. What are your thoughts about this?
- I am looking for honesty.
- I would like you to write down what is going on in your mind.
- I sense that there is an inside joke. Should I be enlightened?

Listening well can help the trainer select action and reaction activities. The third type of group-energizing activities provides traction. Just as a tire tread provides traction for a car on an icy road, the activities of writing, reflecting, and applying provide traction for the learner. They help learners get a grip on concepts.

For example, if you are teaching a particular approach for employee communication, giving time for writing scripts or dialogues is important. You can also ask participants to write something and then share it with a partner. Writing anchors thoughts; sharing encourages feedback and further application. Other writing activities include self-descriptions, letters to oneself, postcards to oneself, and journal writing.

Incubation is an important step in the creative process, and learners need time to reflect. Senge (1990) writes about ever-decreasing reflection time:

> It is easy to blame this . . . lack of time for reflection on organizational pressures but research is beginning to suggest otherwise. We have conducted numerous experiments to study managers' learning habits. Surprisingly, these experiments show that even when there is ample time for reflection, most managers do not reflect carefully on their actions. Typically managers in the experiments adopt a strategy, then as soon as the strategy starts to run into problems, they switch to another strategy. In a simulated four-year exercise, managers may run through three to six different strategies, without once examining why a strategy seems to be failing. Apparently, the 'ready, fire, aim,' atmosphere of American corporations has been fully assimilated and internalized by those who live in that atmosphere.

Reflection is one gift that the trainer can give in a classroom through a period of required silence. Thought can be stimulated by art postcards or stories; participants can reflect on how they relate to the issue at hand.

Application exercises provide traction that brings learning home to the job and to personal experiences. For example, if your group is examining causes for conflict in the organization, participants can begin by writing ideas on Post-it notes, one per note. Next, they reflect silently in groups, organizing the notes on a flipchart. Finally, in large-group discussion, they apply the information by citing the major conflict categories and what they may mean.

Perception, action, reaction, and traction all contribute to energizing a group. Lack of energy, however, is only one group problem. Other group situations also call for careful listening and quick thinking.

HOW CAN YOU LISTEN TO ADAPT TO THE NUANCES OF THE GROUP?

Trainers often need to listen and adapt to the education, experience, and attitude levels of the group. Sometimes the group has more in common than expected; sometimes it is more diverse. For example, if a group consists of all managers, the learning environment is often very different than with a group that includes managers and their staff. Current events often affect a group. Corporate mergers and changes can occur overnight, greatly influencing a learning event.

Remember, in any of these situations, be spontaneous and think impromptu. Most trainers are extremely well organized. To think impromptu, they need to disorganize! One way to think impromptu is to give up some control. Careful listening may tell you to diverge from your original agenda. This can be difficult to do, but if you are appropriately focused on learner outcomes, you will be motivated to be spontaneous.

DELEGATION EXPERTS

A hospital was going through major changes in staffing and job roles. I was assigned to teach delegation skills to a group of very experienced nurses who were feeling defensive about the changes. Quickly, I perceived that they preferred to ask practical questions of their superior, who happened to be in the class, rather than listen to me about delegating. Consequently, I allowed them a half-hour of questions and answers with their superior. Later, I asked them to generate their own delegation models based on their years of experience. Their models were well thought-out, and although I had sacrificed about 45 minutes of the original lesson plan, I gained a more informed, less defensive group.—C.M.

You may also need to adapt activities to meet different education levels. Imagine that you are leading an interpersonal skills course for an entire manufacturing organization from the shop floor to middle managers. You are discussing behavior styles. How would you adapt your questions about their behavior styles? For the more basic level, you may ask, "What are your style's strengths and weaknesses?" Adapted for management, the question may be, "How does your style accommodate a new project with a tight deadline?" Careful listening will tell you if the group needs to be challenged.

Listening can help you rethink how you use games. Certain groups of employees like playing games more than others do. Women, people under 40, and sales and marketing personnel tend to be more enthusiastic about games than men, people over 40, and engineers. Listen to the group and alter a game to make it comfortable for the group or just skip it entirely.

Listening can tell you how to lead a role play. Trainers who can think impromptu can vary the role-play approach on the spot. For example, triad (groups of three) role plays are good when most participants can work well independently, but fishbowl (one role play observed by the group) works better when many group members need encouragement. You can also facilitate fishbowl role plays using team consultants. The team is allowed to help the players at any time: The players can call a time-out to get help, or the team members can yell, "Cut!" to gain time to give the player suggestions.

You may need to edit content on an impromptu basis. Many trainer guides are packed with too much content. Occasionally, however, a session can zoom by and you will find that you need to stretch the content. To speed up a session, try these ideas:

- Delete certain visuals.
- Use a visual instead of a wordy handout.
- Consolidate 10 items into three major items.
- Omit a job-specific example to alleviate an intense discussion.
- Delete a video or a section of a video.
- Ask for a large-group discussion instead of small breakout groups.

To slow down a session, consider these suggestions:

* Give the first three items in a list of 10 and have participants create the rest.
* Ask for each participant to share a personal story.
* Have small groups discuss and report something.

Thinking on your feet is easier for some people than others. Trainers can use basic improvisational concepts to help adapt to groups and situations. Here are a few tips that you might learn in an improvisation class:

* *Say "Yes, and . . ." instead of "Yes, but . . ."* If someone gives you an idea, do not argue it but build on it. Here is an example: An interpersonal class is discussing how to handle a difficult co-worker. The group is eliciting good suggestions until a participant suggests, "Be abusive and aggressive right back to him. I learned that in the army and that's the only way it will stop." Obviously, this is not a recommended approach, so the trainer can say, "Yes, and you need to be prepared for the defensive reaction that will result from your aggressive approach. What will you do then?"
* *Be inspired by others' ideas.* All the wisdom in the world is not in the trainer guide. Participants remember what they say more than what you say, anyway.
* *Do not be afraid of silence.* When asking a question, it is important to allow silence; someone will most likely respond. One Chicago-based diversity trainer does a wonderful job of pausing after she asks, "What questions do you have?" She knows that people are often reluctant to contribute on diversity issues.
* *Conflict is not as interesting as agreement; find agreement.* It is important to agree with each other. When improvising an imaginary scene, if a scene partner turns to you and says, "Boy, this elevator is slow," you would not want to respond, "What do you mean this elevator? We're in line at the movies!" You would want to say something like, "I know what you mean. Do you think they'll ever get it repaired?" A trainer can seek to build agreement in situations rather than the conflict.
* *Less is more. Keep it simple.* A trainer's wisdom in front of a group is tied directly to his or her ability to listen. Experienced trainers will say that the longer that they are trainers, the less they talk. We can all try to remember TLC: talk less and care.

ARE YOU READY TO LISTEN TO LEARN?

This chapter has covered the skills involved in listening and the margin notes that trainers can make while listening to help advance the learning. To wrap up this chapter, take self-assessment 7-2 to see how you are listening to learn.

Listening is a skill that anyone can learn. As a trainer, you do not need to be a topic expert to be able to facilitate learning. You do not really need to have years of experience. Nevertheless, you do need to listen and to be very interpersonally aware. You need to be an observation expert. You need to keep writing in the margins.

Self-Assessment 7-2.
Listening to learn.

Directions: Before your next learning initiative, check to see if you are prepared to listen to learn. Ask yourself the questions below.

Analyze listening barriers.

Have I planned adequately to eliminate listening barriers?

What types of barriers will challenge me physically, intellectually, emotionally?

What particular person(s) will present a listening barrier for me?

What situation(s) will present a listening barrier for me?

Select techniques to overcome barriers.

What can I do ahead of time to meet with people to alleviate the barriers?

What responses or questions can I plan to alleviate the barriers?

What skills will I use when I meet these barriers: attend, restate, check perception?

Listen in difficult situations.

What potential difficulties will surround this learning?

Will there be any red flags or hot buttons to consider?

Are current events affecting this learning situation?

How can I plan to respond nondefensively to difficulties?

Whom should I meet with in advance to help me respond effectively?

Listen to energize the group.

Am I ready to use my perception to be honestly aware of what the group is telling me?

Have I planned at least one activity that uses action?

Have I planned questions to get a reaction?

Do I have a unique activity to achieve traction?

Listen to adapt to the nuances of the group.

What are the demographics of the group?

Am I prepared to respond to the needs of different age levels?

Am I prepared to respond to different experience levels?

Am I prepared to respond to different education levels?

Think impromptu.

Have I found places in my agenda where I can adapt?

Have I considered where I can allow silence?

Am I ready to put my ego aside and be inspired by others?

Can I TLC (talk less and care)?

8

Ask Great Questions

Why are you reading this chapter? What do you hope to gain professionally by reading this particular topic? What specific skills do you wish to improve? How does this topic fit into your overall learning goals? By asking yourself questions such as these, you can link the topic to your own specific learning needs. Asking great questions—whether you are doing a self-assessment or working with participants—is a vital training skill.

Questions do not receive much credit on the scale of greatness. You often hear about great presentations, great visual effects, great games, great classes, great trainers, great videos, great case studies, great toys to relax participants, and even great handouts. How often do you hear that a trainer asked great questions? Yet, the art of asking great questions is one of the most underrated and important skills for trainers. Why?

PARTNERSHIP

The most fundamental answer is partnership. When you ask a participant a question and really want to know his or her answer, you are enfolding him or her into a partnership. You do not assume that you know how he or she feels, believes, or thinks about a particular subject. You are implicitly saying, "Your ideas are important to me." You are reaching out your hand and inviting the learner to be your partner in the inquiry. You are opening the communication gate and encouraging him or her to step forward and join you in finding an answer. Together, you become actively engaged in the quest for answers. Communication truly goes both ways. When you ask for ideas and listen to learn from the answers, you become a learner partner in the search for knowledge. You become intimate with the learner's needs and wants.

QUESTIONING SKILLS OUTSIDE THE CLASSROOM

One way to demonstrate the importance that you should attach to questioning skills is to be aware of its usage outside the classroom. For example, experienced, successful salespeople know that probing skills are the key to understanding customer needs. They perfect the art of asking great questions and listening keenly to the answers customers provide. Less skilled salespeople tend to talk more and question less, a concept that has been memorialized with the slogan: "If you're tellin', you ain't sellin'!" Skilled negotiators ask questions to determine overlapping interests and move antagonists beyond the positions they are stuck in. Counselors and therapists hone their questioning skills so that their clients may discover important insights for themselves. Perhaps you were trained in one of these professions. If you were, the art of questioning comes quite naturally. Skilled learning leaders elevate the art of asking great questions as these professionals have.

OPEN-ENDED QUESTIONS

Professionals who are skilled at questioning know that open-ended questions should normally be used to elicit the most information. An open-ended question cannot be answered by a simple *yes* or *no*. For example, if you were asked if you had a good vacation, you would logically answer *yes* or *no*. If someone asked you how you enjoyed your vacation, you would be more likely to answer with a longer, more expansive reply. Open-ended questions usually begin with *what, where, why, how, when, tell me about,* or *please explain.* Capable questioners use open-ended questions at the beginning of dialogue (verbal or written) when they wish to elicit as much information as possible. Closed-ended questions are used to probe for specific information, often as a follow-up query.

WHY ASK THE QUESTION AT ALL?

Besides the open versus closed distinction, it is equally important to move beyond technique and ask: Why are you asking this question? Several motives may lie behind the probe. The most superficial, perhaps, is just to encourage the other person or persons to participate in the discussion.

SUPERFICIAL QUESTIONING

Early in my training career, I had a tendency to use warm-up activities for the sole purpose of getting students involved and participating. I might throw out a topic and ask the group for a definition. For example, I might ask them to define a word like service. As people answered my question, I would jot down their answers on a flipchart. Then, I would ignore their answers and tell them the real answer, my definition. This is an example of using a question to elicit superficial involvement and participation. I wasn't really interested in learning from their definitions.

When this type of token involvement is the primary objective for using questions, students soon become very cynical about responding. Yet, many trainers believe good facilitation means merely asking questions for the sake of participation only. Such activity creates a very narrow outcome. —B.L.

Great questions have the potential to produce great results, including the following:

- Creating learner partnerships by enhancing your knowledge and the knowledge of other participants. When the trainer asks for ideas, is he or she listening politely to facilitate participation or really listening to learn?
- Eliciting the "eureka" effect, or a significant moment outcome, by helping the learner step back and reflect on his or her behavior, goals, or values. When the trainer asks participants what they noticed about their own listening, participants may recognize a listening pattern they like or one they wish to change.
- Encouraging generative learning by establishing a process for learners to create their own answers and models. When learners are asked to think about times they received extraordinary service, the trainer is helping the learner create his or her own model of service excellence.
- Empowering committed action by encouraging the learner to take action back at work. When the trainer provides an opportunity to make a commitment to change behavior, it gives the learner a platform for applying insights in the real world.
- Acknowledging talent by enabling a team of learners to realize the progress they have made. Whenever a learning leader asks a team of learners to summarize their progress, it provides for positive self-regard.
- Recognizing each person's unique voice and experience by providing an opportunity for people to tell their personal stories and recollections. When learning leaders provide a forum for people to share their stories, a tapestry of diversity is revealed.
- Stimulating a learning partnership by fostering joint ownership of a learning experience. When the trainer asks the learning team to develop ground rules for itself, self-management and self-reliance has been accomplished.

USING QUESTIONING IN TRAINING

Asking great questions involves four important concepts. First, recognize that questioning is a critical competency for learning leaders, certainly as important as presentation skills. Second, use questioning to establish partnerships among all the participants in a learning environment. When you ask and listen as a learning partner, true partnership has been achieved. Third, use open-ended questions most of the time to encourage the receiver to speak abundantly. Fourth, make your questions purposeful to move beyond mere participation for greater potential outcomes. Now, it is possible to apply these four concepts to specific training situations.

Needs Analysis

Performing a needs analysis answers the question of what you should do as the learning leader to provide what is wanted and needed by the client (Stadius, 1999; Pfeiffer & Ballew, 1988). Although many valid approaches exist, in this chapter the one-on-one interview method is used to demonstrate the power of questioning in needs analysis. One advantage of this method is that it allows more in-depth, probing questions. People are often more open in a one-on-one setting.

Before you conduct one-on-one interviews, you should be clear about your objectives in using this method. This approach

- allows you to target your training to meet your client's specific needs.
- enables you to establish a relationship with the learners before the class begins.
- uncovers cultural and organizational issues that may affect training outcomes.
- permits you to explain your training philosophy and methods.
- gives you an opportunity to check out assumptions you have made about the organization or client group.

Preliminary assumptions about what a client needs are frequently based on initial conversations with the person who is requesting your services. That person might be an HR professional or line manager. As an example, team building is frequently advocated as a remedy when the problem may lie with one individual—and that individual may be the line manager who requested the intervention! This would never be uncovered without a thorough needs analysis. The proper remedy may be one-on-one coaching with the line manager and not a team building process.

All needs analysis objectives, including checking out initial assumptions, help establish partnership. The person being interviewed is jointly creating the training program with you. It is useful to acknowledge this joint creation during the interview session.

Needs Analysis Setup

A quiet, private conference room provides a good environment for needs analysis interviews. In addition to your outline of questions, bring plenty of pencils and paper to record answers. Usually, 45 minutes is about the right length of time. If you are training a group of 50 people, interviewing 10 or 20 percent of the group will provide a good sample. You can usually interview eight persons in a day.

At the beginning of the session, introduce yourself, thank the person for taking time to help create the training program, and emphasize that his or her answers will be held in strict confidence. The responses, you explain, will be combined with others to paint a montage of training needs. Then, encourage the person to ask questions and to expand upon any of the topics covered during the session. In addition, give the person a brief description of your background, including how you became associated with the organization. You will discover that sharing a little personal information up front encourages the person to be open and forthright during the session. As in many communication situations, setting it up right produces the best outcomes.

Needs Analysis Questions

Part of establishing an open climate is asking benign questions about the interviewee's background during the first phase of the interview. Length of time with the company, reason for career selection, name of department and position title, brief description of job duties—those types of questions are appropriate.

Throughout the session, open-ended questions should be designed to get at specific subject matter areas and reveal general information about the organization's culture and climate that might affect training success. Different question formats can be used for team building, sales, management development, presentation skills, and so forth.

Figure 8-1 is a sample needs analysis format for management training. The questions listed would be used in a flexible, creative fashion. You would never use all the questions listed in such an outline. When an individual is verbose and open, you may only need three or four of the planned questions.

The real art is in probing beneath the first answer for deeper meaning and for hidden assumptions and listening intently for openings in the person's answers. Here is an example of an exchange that might occur during a needs analysis interview:

Trainer: "What kind of support do you receive for your job?" (planned question from format)

Interviewee: "It's okay."

Trainer: "What do you mean by 'okay'?"

Interviewee: "Well, I don't like my manager's attitude."

Trainer: "Oh?"

Interviewee: "Yeah, my manager won't let me do anything without scrutinizing every word or detail. It's very frustrating. I'm not used to having a manager who supervises me so closely."

Trainer: "Have you discussed this with your manager?"

Interviewee: "No. I'm too scared to do it. I'm not very assertive when it comes to speaking up."

Trainer: "Would assertiveness training help you deal with these uncomfortable situations?"

Interviewee: "Maybe. I need something to help me stand up for what I think is right. This is something that I do all the time. I'm really tired of being a doormat! My friends keep telling me to stand up for myself more."

Trainer: "Thanks for being so open with me. I will definitely consider adding assertiveness to our team building agenda."

By following up with second-level questions, the trainer in this needs analysis dialogue uncovered two important issues. First, the trainer has revealed a possible need for assertiveness training for the team building program being designed. If several people mention the same concern during needs interviews, assertiveness will certainly be included. Second, she has discovered a possible control problem with the manager. Again, if this issue is disclosed during other interviews, the trainer may suggest one-on-one coaching for the manager. This second need is an unforeseen area that is outside the original learning objective (team building). Finding such unanticipated training needs is often a result of using great questions to probe for deeper meaning. Following the needs analysis interviews, a brief report could be written summarizing findings and recommending appropriate human performance interventions.

Figure 8-1. Needs analysis questions designed primarily for managers and supervisors.

Preliminary Remarks

1. Thank the person for taking time for the interview.
2. Explain confidential nature of the interview.
3. Talk about how the information will be used.

Interview Questions (to be used flexibly with follow-up probes as needed)

1. Name:

    Title:

    Length of time with company:

    Length of time in current position:

    Experience before current position:
2. Please describe your primary job responsibilities.
3. What personal rewards do you get at work?
4. How were you trained for your management responsibilities?
5. Please tell me about some distractions or barriers at work that keep you from getting your primary job responsibilities completed.
6. What are some positive aspects of your job? What are some negative aspects?
7. What job functions do you find most enjoyable? What job functions do you find least enjoyable?
8. What would you change about your job if you could?
9. What kind of support do you receive for your job?
10. How does your job fit into the overall success of the company?
11. What do think is most important about your work? What do think is least important about your work?
12. What behaviors are rewarded in your department?
13. How do you encourage your staff to provide excellent production quality and productivity?
14. How do you support your staff on a day-to-day basis?
15. Tell me about a challenging situation one of your staff handled recently. How did the person deal with the situation? Were you satisfied with the result? Do you think the other person was satisfied with the result? Was this typical? Please explain.
16. How would you describe the overall atmosphere in your department?
17. What gives you the most satisfaction at work?
18. If we were designing a management training program just for you, what would you want included?
19. What do you think your team needs with respect to management training?
20. Is there anything else you would like to share that we have not covered?
21. How do you feel right now about this interview?

In some instances, you may decline not to take any action. Why? If the interview sessions indicate that the potential participants are not ready to learn or confront problems, the training may be wasted. It takes courage to decline to do work for someone. Nevertheless, it might be the right thing for you and the organization you are supporting. Honesty and maturity are needed to make these tough decisions.

TOO MUCH HOSTILITY

A *few years ago, a hospital asked me to do some team building with several rehabilitation departments. When I conducted the needs analysis interviews, I was shocked by the hostility and conflict that existed between the departments. One person even said she would walk over a person who was dying from the other department. I decided that the timing was not right for a successful intervention. Two years later, I did work with the departments after some necessary leadership and personnel changes were made. Training is not always the answer*—B.L.

Asking Questions Before the Training

By asking questions before the training, you can help participants think about a topic in a personal, reflective fashion. Generally, one or two weeks before the training give enough lead time. Today, email can transmit the prework. Keeping prework brief and personal helps ensure that participants complete it. Indicating on the prework that the participant's answers will be used during the seminar also ensures completion. Good prework also provides an emotional link to the topic of the seminar or workshop. When such a connection is established it reinforces the participant's own commitment to learning and growth. Figure 8-2 offers a set of

Figure 8-2. "Speak Up" seminar prework.

To prepare for this seminar, please complete the items below and bring this form with you to the seminar. Your answers will be used during the seminar.

1. Describe your overall attitude about speaking in front of groups.

2. Please list specific presentation skills you wish to improve at the seminar (projecting, organizing the talk, using visual aids, overcoming nervousness, etc.)

3. List the personal benefits you would receive if you were a powerful speaker:

4. Please think of two possible business-related topics for a 10- to 15-minute presentation to be delivered during the seminar. These subjects should be persuasive and not purely informational. Do not prepare your talk; merely consider two topics you could present and list them here.

sample questions to help prepare learners for a presentations skills class entitled "Speak Up."

Opening or Launch Phase

You can use prework questions and answers effectively during the opening phase of your program by having participants share them. The following are the most important questions to ask participants to share:

- *What is your attitude or experience with respect to the topic?* To reveal this perspective, you might inquire about the person's real-life experiences. For example, for technical training you could ask for software programs the person has mastered (figure 8-2, question 1).
- *What do you hope to gain by taking this program?* This could be listed as the learner's objective, goal, or improvement area for the course (figure 8-2, question 2).
- *What benefits will you realize if you improve or change your behavior?* This question helps the person begin to think about how to apply new skills or approaches after the seminar concludes (figure 8-3, question 3).

One way to encourage learners to share such information in class is to fold these questions into a get-acquainted activity. Pairs of participants or small groups at tables can talk about these items with each other. Recorders at the tables or trainers with smaller groups can capture individual improvement areas and post them on flipcharts or electronic boards. This helps the trainer and participants focus on what is important. Being learner-centered, the trainer can alter the course direction to meet the participants' needs as revealed in these opening questions. For example, suppose you are facilitating a program on selling skills. In the opening activity, most of the participants indicated a need to become better at closing sales. You can adjust the program to focus on this identified need by devoting more time to discussion and practice of various closing methods.

Facilitating Classroom Learning

Using questions for stimulating dialogue is as old as the Socratic method. As stressed before, these probing methods should be used to build partnership between the learning leader and learners. Everyone becomes a learning partner in such a climate for learning. To create such an atmosphere, you must be a model yourself. Senge (1990) speaks of the need for the leader to be committed to his or her own personal mastery: "The core leadership strategy is simple: be a model. Commit yourself to your own personal mastery. Talking about personal mastery may open people's minds somewhat, but actions always speak louder than words. There's nothing more powerful you can do to encourage others in their quest for personal mastery than to be serious in your own quest."

Being serious about your own search for knowledge includes being willing to have your own views challenged in the classroom. Trainers often talk about being open to other viewpoints. In real classroom situations, however, how often do they become defensive when students call their authority or views into question? To be a model means to be truly open.

Within this context of openness and mutual exploration, several questioning methods can facilitate learning:

- *Overhead question.* This is a question directed at the entire class. For example, in a customer service class you may ask: "What do you think is the correct way to approach an angry customer?"
- *Debrief question.* This question may be used to stimulate self-exploration. For example, you could ask learners to reflect on what they noticed about their own speaking and listening after completing an experiential activity in the classroom.
- *Application question.* This type of question may be used to encourage a participant to think about applying an insight when he or she returns to the "real world." If someone said, "I should really listen more attentively to my staff," the trainer could respond by saying, "That's an excellent idea, Bob. Would you like to make a commitment to do that when you return to work?" If Bob responded in the affirmative, you could help him explore ways to accomplish that goal. If he were open to help, you could also ask the class for suggestions.
- *One-to-one question.* This question is directed at one individual for response. If you notice someone is frowning, for example, you may ask, "Mary, you seem to be troubled by this discussion. What's on your mind?"
- *Redirected question.* This question is used to redirect a question that has been posed to the trainer. He or she redirects the question to the entire class for an answer. This allows for greater participation and prevents the trainer from becoming the sole source for answers. For example, you can redirect by saying, "Bob has asked an interesting question about paid leave. Does anyone here know what the company policy is on this subject?"
- *Written response.* This question combines overhead and one-to-one methods. It has the advantage of giving everyone an opportunity to speak, and it allows participants time to think of a response. For example, you may use it during a "brag session," during which you instruct the learners to get a piece of paper and briefly write about a recent time when they made a difference in someone's life. After a few minutes, call on each person to share his or her answer with the class or their small group.

After the Class

After someone returns from a learning experience, questions may be used to help the person apply her or his new skills or knowledge on the job. For example, managers of returning staff could ask:

- What did you learn about yourself at the seminar?
- What new skills will you be trying as a result of your training?
- How can I support you in applying these new approaches?
- What ideas can you share at our next staff meeting that could help us all?

Learning leaders should expand their arena of responsibility to include such learning debriefings. Trainers may also include follow-up sessions to debrief people on their progress, or trainers may elect to teach managers how to conduct such sessions. Learning leaders need to use questioning methods to encourage committed action after a learning event. When participants know that they will be part of a follow-up or debriefing process—conducted by either the manager or the trainer—transfer of learning to the job increases substantially.

BUILD YOUR QUESTIONING TALENT

Questions are at the heart of learning. When you use questions skillfully, you provide a platform for inquiry. It all begins with you. To become intimate with the organization and people you are serving, you ask questions to determine their needs. During needs analysis interviews, you are not only discovering training needs, you are also modeling inquiry skills and forging learning partnerships. You are saying to your future learning partners, "I don't have all the answers. I require your insights to design a class that meets your needs." If you skip this essential step, you risk disaster. Then, throughout the learning partnership you continue to use questions to provide a spacious meadow for learning. As the classroom phase closes, you use questions to help your learning partners apply their wisdom, knowledge, and skills. For this reason, the seemingly unglamorous business of questions is worth mastering.

Self-assessment 8-1 touches on the main points in this chapter. Taking a few minutes to complete this activity will also encourage you to apply these questioning principles and practices.

Self-Asssessment 8-1.
Twenty-two questions about questions.

Directions: Check the box that most closely reflects your use of questioning techniques.

Do you...	Yes	No	Need Improvement
recognize the importance of developing questioning skills?			
frequently use open-ended questions to facilitate learning?			
encourage participants to question your methods and ideas?			
ask questions to learn from your participants?			
help learners discover answers for themselves?			
let participants generate their own models?			
empower learners to take committed action after the class?			
acknowledge the wisdom and savvy of participants?			
provide opportunities for participants to tell their unique stories?			
use needs analysis questions to target client training?			
explain your philosophy and methods during needs analysis interviews?			
develop rapport with learners before the training?			
check out your assumptions about clients during the needs analysis process?			
remember to establish rapport during the opening phase of needs analysis interviews?			
use follow-up probes to dig deeper when questioning learners?			
create participant prework that provides an emotional link to the topic to be taught?			
develop prework questions that encourage personal growth?			
model openness in your quest for knowledge in the classroom?			

continued on page 98

Self-Asssessment 8-1.
Twenty-two questions about questions (continued).

Do you...	Yes	No	Need Improvement
debrief experiential activities to maximize learning?			
ask questions to encourage after class application of ideas?			
use written and verbal questions to enhance communication?			
structure follow-up activities to encourage committed action?			

9

FACILITATE
TEAM LEARNING

The effective learning leader uses his or her natural style to listen powerfully and ask great questions. When these skills are used wisely, the result is a team learning together. This is how team learning looks: *The door is ajar, and you peek in. The participants are leading the discussion themselves, listening actively, disagreeing firmly yet politely, referring to both concepts and real-life scenarios, laughing at each other's stories, and occasionally referring a question back to . . . wait a minute . . . who's that? . . . oh yes, the trainer.*

How do you apply your natural style and your listening and probing skills to establish this natural balance between learners and trainer? You facilitate team learning by focusing on eight critical dimensions:

- team atmosphere
- team values
- participation patterns
- shared leadership
- task/maintenance
- alignment
- communication patterns
- logistical variables.

Before exploring each dimension, you need to understand the term *team learning*. First, a team is small group of people working together toward a common purpose for their mutual benefit. In learning settings, the ideal size for such a team is four to six participants. Nevertheless, you often facilitate learning teams that are larger. Organizations cannot always afford to train staff in groups of four to six. In addition, you may be asked to facilitate an intact group, such as a department. Generally, you find yourself training eight to 12 people at one sitting. Therefore, when larger groups are being trained, it is often helpful to break them into smaller learning units during the training session. The common purpose in a learning team refers to the reason the team has come together: to focus on a particular topic. Within that common purpose, each participant on the team has his or her own specific set of expectations. For example, in a time management program, the overall purpose might be "to improve time management skills to help participants achieve their dreams." Within that overall purpose, each participant would bring his or her own goals. One person may want to focus on avoiding procrastination whereas another may want to work on prioritizing daily tasks.

Most importantly, in team learning members realize that they depend upon each other and have agreed on ways to learn together. Your job as facilitator is to create a climate and establish the framework or context for team success. To illustrate team learning, think about your early experiences on a team that learned together. Perhaps it was an athletic team, musical group, or theatrical ensemble. What were the elements that made it successful?

Suppose your team was a high school rock band. It worked because of a common set of musical interests—you all liked the same type of music. It was satisfying because you had complementary skills and knowledge—you each played an instrument that contributed to the sound of the whole ensemble. You had a leader who helped rehearse and motivate your band. You held each other accountable for certain levels of performance and for commitments you made to each other. These commitments included rehearsal and performance times, agreed-upon monetary rewards, and role expectations. Roles included booking agent, financial manager, and equipment manager.

Taking this example a step further, assume your musical group accrued certain benefits from working as a team. First, the band benefited from the collective wisdom of the group. Members encouraged each other to contribute musical ideas during rehearsals. Band members gave useful feedback to each other about the musical performance. Second, everyone was involved. All members shared a sense of ownership. Although there was a formal leader, this person shared control and decision making. The team decided which dates to accept, their general monetary terms, and musical selections to play. The leader created a collegial atmosphere. Consequently, the team was aligned as a whole.

That kind of alignment is the hallmark of an effective learning team. As Senge (1990) notes, "Team learning is the process of aligning and developing the capacity of a team to create the results its members truly desire." As a learning leader, you, too, can create the climate and framework for such teamwork in the classroom. The first step is developing and maintaining team atmosphere.

TEAM ATMOSPHERE

You begin nurturing a climate for team learning from the first moment a participant arrives in the classroom. As you shake hands with each participant, introduce yourself, and thank the person for being there, you begin to create a warm and friendly climate. As more people arrive, you do everything to be certain they are comfortable. You indicate where they should put their belongings, ask about their trip to the training site, and share appropriate information about yourself. You smile and laugh naturally, helping put everybody at ease. Building rapport with each participant sets a tone of mutual respect and begins to build a team atmosphere. You also answer concerns about the course informally before the class begins.

These seemingly trivial opening gestures are important first steps. By attending to participant needs, you begin to break down the traditional student-teacher status barrier that could intrude on team learning. The old paradigm of teacher as superior begins to yield to your new role as learning partner. When you make sure that the participants' personal needs are being met, such as telling them where to hang their coats, you signal that you are there to serve. These opening behaviors—seemingly insignificant, socializing, lightweight actions—can make a huge difference in forging an appropriate climate for learning and establishing a learning partnership.

Here is the catch: These goodwill gestures only work when they are authentic and sincere. You really have to want to serve; you must be interested in getting to know each person as a unique human being. If learners perceive these behaviors merely as manipulative techniques, the actions usually backfire. To perform these positive opening moves, you also have to get to the training site early so that all your logistical tasks are completed. That way, you can focus on participants, not on last-minute equipment or room setup. You must also be familiar with your material so that you can avoid hasty reviews of your leader's guide.

The tone you set at the beginning is reflected back, especially from the participants who are normally friendly and warm. Throughout the learning process, you continue to be a friendly and enthusiastic learner, thereby encouraging others to set the same tone. What if someone is hostile although you and most other participants are acting friendly? Experienced learning leaders recognize that participants often come into training programs with some "baggage" from their personal and professional lives. As a result, various behaviors may occur, especially at the beginning of a training event. The participant may be agitated, unfocused, or even rude. Do not take these behaviors personally. Usually, the behavior or outlook reflects issues that the participant is dealing with at work or home. Give the individual time to settle in. Often, a good learning design will help shift the participant into a more cooperative mood. As the learning team members become acquainted with one another during the opening phase of training, personal problems often recede and a more positive attitude develops. If you overreact and attempt to handle or fix the situation too quickly, it can make matters worse. Be patient and trust the process.

There are times, however, when participants continue to act in inappropriate ways. Sometimes a participant may be disruptive: complaining about the training program in a destructive fashion, refusing to participate in any activities or discussions, being overly argumentative, or frequently violating the agreed-upon ground rules. As the learning leader, your main task is to facilitate team learning. When disruptive behavior occurs, it usually poisons the climate for safe and open inquiry. You should take appropriate action as soon as possible, even if doing so is often unpleasant and challenging. If you ignore the situation, you may lose credibility with the team and risk losing focus on team learning objectives. Use the following techniques to minimize or eliminate the distracting influence of such a participant:

- *Maintain a nondefensive stance.* Count to 10 and take a deep breath to maintain your composure. Also, rephrase the question or concern in neutral terms, while still honoring the essence of the question. For example, if a participant says: "I think that's a dumb idea. It certainly won't work in our department!" You could respond by saying, "So, Phil, you believe that idea isn't practical for your unit?"

- *Go back to the ground rules.* Use the ground rules that relate to the unacceptable behavior. You can say something like this: "Remember, Marsha, we agreed to give feedback with 'care and concern' in our ground rules. Please rephrase your feedback using care and concern. Thanks."

- *Use good feedback skills.* When giving feedback to a participant who is being disruptive, use good feedback guidelines: Maintain the person's self-esteem; be specific, not general; give the feedback as soon as possible after the behavior is observed; and provide the feedback in private. For example, instead of saying "You have a terrible attitude, Bob!" you can say "Bob, you frequently interrupt other people when they are talking. This makes it difficult for them to complete their thoughts. Please wait for them to finish their ideas and then you can express yours. Thanks."

- *Let the group assist.* When a training session is not going well and several participants seem upset, try to uncover what is happening beneath the surface. You can say, "Several of you seem very tired and upset today. What's going on?"

- *Let the person vent.* Sometimes it helps to allow some self-expression. Permitting a person to vent for a short period will often help the individual move on and participate as a productive member of the learning team.

- *Talk to the participant privately.* If the disruptive behavior continues, talk with the person at the next break. Gently probe to find out the underlying problem. For example: "Bill, let's talk for a minute. You seem to be upset today. Your angry outbursts are disrupting the class. What seems to be the problem?" If the person refuses to discuss the issue with you it may be necessary to ask him or her to leave.

- *Let the participant decide what to do.* During a private chat, ask the person what should be done. You can say, "Lynn, I understand why you are upset today. The death of your best friend is a very emotional experience. Would you like to continue the training or reschedule at a better time?"

THE ANGRY PARTICIPANT

*A*t a half-day customer service seminar a few years ago, I encountered *the most disruptive behavior ever! Eight participants—all health care providers at a pediatric hospital—were attending the course as part of a hospital-wide effort to improve customer service. One participant, a nurse from the night shift, refused to participate in any classroom activities or listen to anyone in the room. Instead, she read a Stephen King novel during all small-group exercises. When she did speak, she sounded very hostile. I attempted to make small talk during the group activities, but she just kept reading her book.*

Then, I tried to talk to her at the first break, but she timed her coming and going so that she left immediately and came back exactly before the seminar continued. Finally, during another brief break, I found her in the hall. She told me that she had been "forced" to attend by her manager and this had upset her. She said it wasn't personal—she just didn't want to be there. I kept my composure throughout this incident, using it as internal motivation to do a great job no matter what. I never said anything about this situation to anyone outside the class, but her peers complained to their managers, and she didn't attend the follow-up session.

I discovered that such ordeals can strengthen you, instead of pulling you down or forcing you to abandon the other participants. It is all part of being a learning leader.—B.L.

TEAM VALUES

In addition to attending to team atmosphere another important element is team value setting. Values, such as openness, are important for learning team success. How do you convey them to the team when you are the facilitator?

First, you must model core values yourself. During the introductory phase of training, invite learners to contribute their ideas. You may say, "I will be sharing my ideas about quality improvement during the next three sessions, but I'm interested in your ideas, too. Many of you have background and experience in this area. We will all be learning from each other. In fact, the best ideas have come from seminar participants like you. I have modified my courses because of suggestions from participants. Let's be a team of learners during our time together!" You can go even further by inviting the learners to challenge your ideas. You might say, "Please feel free to challenge my ideas. I don't have a monopoly on the truth. Over time I have changed or modified my point of view on almost all topics—so your input is welcomed and will be a gift for all of us."

In addition to the important modeling you provide as the class begins, you may convey learning values by talking about your service motto (chapter 5). As you convey your service motto, use personal examples and stories to provide interest and color.

Team values should be reflected in the ground rules, a set of guidelines developed by all members of the learning team for learning together. If your team does not estabish a set of ground rules, you should review your own set of expectations with the team. Some teams end up with an amalgam of the trainer's rules and the learning team's standards. Typical rules include logistical guidelines, such as starting and ending times. Ways to speak and listen to each other are often incorporated. For example, agreeing to listen openly to others or being open to other participants' ideas may be established as a ground rule. Ground rules that encourage full participation are often set down, too. To encourage self-monitoring of the ground rules, a keeper of the ground rules may be appointed. When anyone on the learning team strays from the rules—including you—this person is empowered to interrupt and gently redirect the offending participant. If your program runs over several days or months, you may want to rotate this "grounds keeper" role.

Team values are established at the beginning of a training program by articulating your vision for the session through your service motto, modeling these values for the learners, and by establishing ground rules with the learning team. You may use all three approaches or whichever suits your natural style.

PARTICIPATION PATTERNS

How do you recognize if these values are being expressed during your training program? One way is to observe the level of participation in the team. Simply noticing how well the learners are participating is helpful. Who are the high and low participators? Are there any cliques or subgroups that are distracting from group work? Assuming you want maximum participation in the learning process, several methods can encourage involvement:

One technique that maximizes wisdom sharing has each participant write down, then share answers with the learning team. Give participants time to reflect on a topic, write down their ideas, and then share these insights with the learning team. Another method borrowed from a team building workshop is asking the group, "Please take two minutes to jot down your initial thoughts and feelings as a member of a new team. You will be sharing your answers with the class."

Assuming that all learners have had opportunity to consider the question at hand, either through prework or a time of reflection, call upon each person for input. Calling on participants individually keeps each participant alert and involved. You may ask a participant, "Jill, what has been your experience in this area?" Then, call on each person in the group to add their own input to the inquiry. Use this technique with care. Some participants may balk at being "put on the spot." One way to soften this approach is to allow participants to "pass" whenever they cannot think of an idea to contribute.

Inclusion is enhanced by an approach that is universally recognized for its effectiveness: experiential learning. When you use this learning-by-doing approach, it is best to create realistic activities or structured experiences. When you design role plays, case studies, or virtual reality games, use situations that mirror real-life scenarios from the learners' lives. Whenever feasible, ask learners to design their own scenarios on the spot. For example, during a sales training program, ask participants to design role plays that use their own products and services. Always debrief or process observed behaviors after such structured activities. Following a sales training role play, for example, ask the main participants which closing techniques were effectively used and which behaviors could have been more effective. To ensure that each role play is debriefed thoroughly, assign observers to watch for such patterns during role plays and to report their observations after the activity.

Most experiential activities involve breaking a larger learning team into temporary small groups. While the *ideal* class size is four to size participants, you are frequently called on to facilitate larger teams for reasons of cost or to keep an intact department together. Certainly, eight to 12 participants is a workable class size, especially when you design breakout groups throughout your program. Oftentimes, participants are more comfortable sharing their ideas in such settings. Shy and less assertive participants often open up in small groups. From pairs (dyads) to groups of six (sextets), such interaction often produces excellent participation and team insights. Dividing into small groups also reduces informal subgrouping as you split people into different configurations.

Forced consensus on a topic often yields good group work. For example, as part of a team building program you may ask, "Based on your homework from last night, reach a consensus as a group on the top three qualities of an effective team."

All of these small-group processes—forced consensus, experiential work in small groups, or calling on each participant for input—help draw all learners into the learning partnership by maximizing participation. Sharing leadership also has a positive effect on participation.

SHARED LEADERSHIP

As you are driving to the training site, it is important to remind yourself that you are a learning partner, not a star entertainer. Chicago HR consultant Mary Jane Brown (2000) brings home the point: "As a facilitator the most important thing I try to keep in mind as I prepare to work with a group is that the work is not about me. I am simply a guide for the group to get done whatever it is they need/want to achieve. When a facilitator becomes the center of the effort, the best that he or she can accomplish is merely entertainment."

One way to avoid becoming the "center of the effort" is to share leadership functions during the learning event. Following the 30/70 rule keeps you from dominating the training session. Speak about 30 percent of the time in the classroom. Participants should fill the remaining 70 percent of the airtime. This may be difficult to maintain in some training situations and topics, but the rule often helps to maintain a good balance of trainer-participant input.

You can also share the spotlight by sharing leadership responsibilities. After a small group has reached a decision, let each group spokesperson report the team's results in front of the room, sharing the spotlight with you. Another way to reinforce that your participants' ideas are as valid as yours is to publish their work. Have their ideas typed, reproduced, and included in their manual or materials. Use the same design (borders, fonts, colors, and so forth) to make the point that their concepts and insights have equal status with your published ideas. Normal practice is to post group ideas on flipcharts and discard the sheets at the end of the day. What does that say about their relative importance?

Besides giving equal status to the learners' views, shared leadership also implies letting participants lead discussions. Discussion leaders should be encouraged, often via ground rules, to include everyone in discussions and problem solving. Encouraging others by opening the gate and inviting them to participate is a legitimate role for both you and the learners who are facilitating discussions. Someone leading a discussion can open the gate by asking, "Mary, we've heard from other folks, what do you think about this matter?" At times, a facilitator (either you or another learning team leader) may have to close the gate gently thus, "Bill, I appreciate your willingness to share your views, but we have to move on to the next topic."

TASK/MAINTENANCE BALANCE

The need to open or close discussion usually reflects a perception about task/maintenance balance. The task is the topic or subject you are discussing. Maintenance refers to maintaining the morale of people on the learning team.

Examples of staying on task include beginning and ending on time, being clear about your purpose and learning objectives, and providing clear instructions for various class activities. Maintenance or morale factors include how people are reacting to the material being discussed, overall climate of the team, and handling the individual concerns of participants. You need to find a natural balance between meeting the overall team purpose and meeting the needs of individual learners. For example, during a discussion of conflict resolution methods, one learner may want the group to handle a real conflict he or she is experiencing. If time permits, you should weave this personal concern into the program. On the other hand, you must also focus on covering several topics before the session concludes. You must balance what the entire class needs with individual problems and issues that may arise.

ALIGNMENT

After conveying learning values, it is important to observe how these values are being implemented. To what extent are participants maintaining the ground rules? You or the grounds keeper may need to remind people gently about the learning framework that has been created for their benefit.

COMMUNICATION PATTERNS

How everyone speaks and listens to each other is another important indicator of team learning effectiveness. Does everyone speak through you as in a courtroom where all parties have to speak through the judge, or are they encouraged to speak directly to each other? Is the tone friendly, cooperative, or competitive?

Are learners listened to respectfully even if their views are at odds with the prevailing, politically correct thinking? Maintaining a spirit of inquiry is reflected in individual speech and listening behaviors. When people are cut off or ignored (sometimes referred to as a "plop"), how is that handled? Do people on your learning team ever notice this kind of disrespectful behavior?

The way people present opposing views also indicates whether a spirit of inquiry is present. Do they do so in a hostile way or do they build on what the other person has said? The concept of "builds" originated at Quaker meetings. According to Megginson, at such gatherings, much of the verbal communication consists of building on other people's ideas: " . . . that is, they take account of what the previous speaker has said, and add to it, rather than disagreeing or going off on an unrelated tangent" (Harrison, 1983).

In addition to builds, another interesting communication pattern is the degree of transparency evident on the team. Are you sharing personal information appropriately? Too much disclosure closes off discussion. Not enough openness negatively affects trust and information sharing. It can be very helpful if you share personal examples related to the topic at hand. During a self-management program, for example, you may talk about a time when you overcame adversity. On the other hand, talking about an argument you had with your spouse the past week just to get it off your chest would be inappropriate self-disclosure. Modeling openness wisely encourages others to be transparent, too.

LOGISTICAL VARIABLES

Attending to these human interactions is important. The physical space you use also affects learning results. Configuring a room in a traditional, classroom format tends to favor an instructor-to-student communication pattern. On the other hand, using U-shaped, round, or conference tables enhances small-group communication.

If you want to encourage a playful environment, place toys and other playful objects at each participant's place. Music can also help put learners in certain moods. A word of caution: Too much reliance on these techniques, commonly associated with accelerated learning methods, may distract you and your learning team from more important concerns. If you want to maximize person-to-person interaction, keep your energy and focus on matters that relate directly to facilitating team learning.

PUT YOUR LEARNING LEADERSHIP SKILLS TO THE TEST

Facilitating team learning takes years of practice and experience. No matter how seasoned you are, continual improvement is always possible and desirable. As you lead your next training session, use self-assessment 9-1 to reflect on how effectively you build learning partnerships with the learners.

Self-Assessment 9-1.

How effective are the learning partnerships that you establish?

Directions: To assess your facilitation skills and the team dynamics that influence learning, complete the following observation sheet by writing down your answers or by mentally observing the following dimensions.

Team Atmosphere	Team Values	Participation Patterns	Shared Leadership
• To what extent is the overall atmosphere friendly and congenial? • To what extent is the overall atmosphere cold and unfriendly? • Who tries to keep the atmosphere friendly and warm? • Are any members hostile toward the team or team learning? • How are conflicts resolved?	• To what extent do team members agree on how they should treat each other? • To what extent are these values observed by team members? • Is there a way to monitor and self-manage these ground rules? • What are the unspoken, hidden values that influence the team?	• To what extent do all team members participate in discussions? • Who are the high and low participants? • Are there any cliques (subgroups) in the team?	• To what extent is leadership shared? • To what extent does the trainer dominate the learning process? • Who are the natural leaders on the learning team? • Do some team members act as gate-openers, inviting others to share their ideas? • Do some team members act as gate-closers, limiting what others say?

Task/Maintenance Balance	Alignment	Communication Patterns	Logistical Variables
• To what extent is the team staying on task, meeting team learning objectives? • To what extent is the team flexible—meeting individual needs as well as overall learning objectives?	• To what extent are participants cooperative and supportive of each other? • Are there any participants who undercut cooperation and team focus?	• What is the direction of the communication: leader-to-group, learner-to-learner, or does all communication go through the learning leader?	• How does the physical environment affect the learning atmosphere (e.g., temperature, room setup, breakout room locations)? • What effect is timing having on the learning process?

- Are there any participants who keep the team focused on its goals?

- What is the tone of the communication: friendly, hostile, open, or closed to others' views?

- To what extent are participants listened to respectfully?

- To what extent are participants encouraged to speak up?

- What is the level of sharing personal issues and concerns? Is it appropriate, too open, too closed, or just right?

- What effect does group size play?

SECTION 3.
HELP LEARNERS APPLY INSIGHTS

10 | FOCUS ON APPLICATION

What is the point of training if learners do not apply their insights on the job? After all, the classroom event is just the beginning. It is the rehearsal stage for the main event—application on the job. This has always been a goal of training and development, but with the increasing trend toward immediate performance response at work, it has become even more essential. As John Cone, vice president of Dell University put it, "The ideal learning event at Dell has a class size of one, lasts five to 10 minutes, and takes place within 10 minutes of when someone recognizes that he or she needs to know something" (Fox, Byrne & Rouault, 1999). Cone's observation typifies the pace of the workplace and the way new generations approach learning. On-the-spot problem solving and networking provide today's employees the answers they need.

In an enlightening study of why 60,000 employees quit their jobs, Interim Services, a survey company, found that employees' loyalty is tied to confidence in their ability to do meaningful work (Olesen, 1999). When they have that confidence, employees are motivated to learn, to become mentees, and to grow. They are saying to employers, "Teach me the things that will keep me employed here."

As a trainer, you lead the way out of the classroom; it is your job to position what comes next, a task that is not as difficult as you may think. You simply help learners use their natural resources conservatively and with appreciation. What are the most ready-to-use learning resources? What will help them focus on application? The three most immediately available natural resources to help learners apply their new insights on the job are the individual, the manager, and the organization. These resources often do not cost a lot of money. They are not usually hard to find. Used wisely, they can be both efficient and effective.

Professional speaker and marketing expert Mark Sanborn, who addresses workplace trends, refers to the term *resources* in his presentations. For example, he encourages salespeople to consider their goods as resources rather than products. Sanborn (1999) explains that today's customers respond to anything that can help them do things more quickly, more productively, and with better quality. His ideas apply to training, too. The key for both trainers and learners is being able to recognize their training resources and to use them.

GLOBAL INSIGHT

Recently, I received a request from the owner of a successful, global direct-mail management company to present the annual kickoff conference for employees. The owner's insight was admirable. He said, "Every year we have this corporate meeting, and we do a workshop or something on communication, and everyone gets revved up. But, as the year goes by, people forget. Arguments and disagreements happen; communication goes downhill. Can you do something to help us do better this year?" In our ensuing discussion, he told me that he had considered job aids and follow-up sessions with managers. I was impressed that he knew of and had considered these important follow-up measures, and I helped him select some appropriate options. Often, company leaders expect the magical, motivational insights of a retreat or conference to last for an entire year. The reality is that they are usually forgotten amidst the chaos and conflict of the workplace.—C.M.

THE INDIVIDUAL AS A RESOURCE

Self-management is essential in every aspect of the workplace today, especially in career management. Ghoshal and Bartlett (1999) state, "Each employee takes responsibility for his or her best in class performance and undertakes to engage in the continuous process of learning that is necessary to support such performance." Today's learners must accept that they are their own best resource. They should be encouraged to evaluate constantly their own ability to perform on the job and not to wait for someone else to do it for them.

Clearly, however, learners do look to other individuals—their managers, coaches, co-workers—for guidance and support. They may look upon managers and coaches as sources of expert advice, and they may see exemplary co-workers as models of star performance. Learners may draw upon their examples so that they can apply relevant concepts to their own jobs.

ASK THE COACH

Following are a few questions that have come through my Website on the subject of coaching in a column called, "Ask the Coach."

Q: What do you do about co-workers who pass the buck?

A: If you work with someone who continually shirks responsibility, it's important to talk to him or her about it. People who have this habit have gotten by with it for too long. Let your temper cool, find a private place, and tell the co-worker that you feel (surprised, frustrated, really mad, and so forth) about the situation and why. Explain how his or her lack of initiative affects your job and your own productivity. If you feel that you need a supervisor present, ask your supervisor if the three of you can meet to talk about job responsibilities. Say, "There must be some confusion . . . " and clarify your job responsibilities on the spot.

Q: Everyone talks about my boss behind her back. I'd like to help her but I'm fairly new.

A: First of all, wait until you have a real grasp of why people are talking. Then, if you feel that there would be a benefit in your boss's knowing about their concerns, approach her about a concern yourself. Don't say, "People are talking about you," but state your own sincere observation, such as, "It seems as if people are quiet during our meetings. Do you have any ideas on how we could be encouraged to express real thoughts and feelings during the meeting?" Eventually, you may be able to discuss the concerns with your boss without putting her on the defensive immediately.

Q: A guy I work with is up for a promotion and he doesn't even know it. The problem is that I think his dress choice and language usage may prevent him from getting it. He acts like "one of the guys from the neighborhood." What can I do?

A: The only person who can really approach him easily about this is his own manager. The manager can say, "Joe, you're doing really well in the organization and, to be promoted, you may want to work with someone to polish your image. It is helpful for all of us to have an objective person help with how we speak and dress. What do you think?" Very few people would say no to corporate-backed image coaching.—C.M.

It's clear that most employees today admire co-workers who do their share of the work and more. They are frustrated when they see ineffective communication, lack of initiative, or unacknowledged performance among their co-workers. Robert Kelley, in his 1998 study of peer-nominated stars at work, found that stars take initiative; they figure out what should get top priority on their to-do lists.

As a trainer, you can encourage learners to self-manage. There are many ways to do this. Perhaps the simplest method is to ask them what they will do next at the conclusion of the learning event. For example, Jerilyn Willin, an organizational development consultant to many global corporations, asks learners to share at the start of training " . . . what they want to take away from their time investment in training" (Willin, 1996). Then, at the completion of the workshop, she takes an important next step: articulating the part they play in achieving their learning goals. Specifically, she asks them to share one action that they are committed to fulfilling in the next 24 hours that will represent new behaviors on the job.

More and more companies are involving learners in professional development programs that include specific follow-up activities and applications. Even in today's busy workplace, learners can be encouraged to focus on applying skills and information. They can keep progress logs and reports. They can complete self-checks to remind them of their goals; the simplest self-checks often work best. For example, Karyn Buxman, a well-known humorist and trainer in the healthcare field, uses a creative sticker to help participants remember to relax. First, she reminds them that when people are stressed, their jaws clench, their teeth grind, and their tongues stick tautly to the roof of their mouths. At the end of the session, she passes out small, transparent stickers that read "Tongue Check" and encourages people to place them on their cars' rearview mirrors to remind them to relax when in traffic.

Stickers, coupons, and easy-to-read messages make great reminders. Another expert in the area of stress, speaker Rita Emmett, passes out small cards that state,

"The person who never makes a MISTAKE probably isn't doing anything." Looking at the card on their desks, learners are reminded that nobody is perfect. At Helene Curtis, trainers sometimes distribute coupons worth 30 minutes of individual coaching and feedback for participants to use before their next presentations. It is the trainer's role to present these tools and promote their use in a manner that encourages learners to use them.

Sometimes, trainers use personal stories or analogies. For example, to help her session participants change behavior, Neale Godfrey (1999), author of several books on financial responsibility, suggests that they "clean out their sock drawers" periodically. Using the analogy of a typical sock drawer with too many unmatched or unworn socks, she suggests making a list similar to this one:

1. Things I want to start but I'm not starting.
2. Things I want to change but I'm not changing.
3. Things I want to stop but I'm not stopping.
4. Things I started but I never completed.
5. Things I want to do but I've never done.

She then asks participants to write an example of each item and decide which ones are the most important in their lives at that moment. Learners easily can use similar checklists to apply to almost any professional learning goal whether it relates to communication, technology, career growth, or teamwork.

The more specific the follow-up activity, the more effective it is. Another activity that works well is an assigned posttraining presentation to the rest of the team to summarize what was learned and how it could be applied to the team's work. This type of follow-up usually involves management approval. Managers are another important resource to the effectiveness of training.

THE MANAGER AS A RESOURCE

Managers as natural resources are much like parents. They are naturally and always present. They are often the reason why learners themselves are there in the first place. Perhaps the manager had a part in hiring or promoting them or asking that they be on their team. Naturally, managers want their people to excel. If their people excel, the manager's life is easier. Why then, are managers some of the most difficult people to involve in training?

Perhaps, like parents, they are just too busy. Perhaps, like parents, they do not feel qualified to comment. Perhaps they do not realize how important their role is. More often than not, they just need help dropping old habits and assuming new roles as coaches and champions of learning.

VISIBLE MANAGERS

When I ask new supervisors to describe the best managers they've ever had, they nearly always mention managers who have the ability to both nurture and to let go. For example, when leading supervisory training for new service supervisors in field operations, trainees of all ages mention *managers who had meaningful, weekly check-in meetings or who met with them occasionally just to talk. They liked managers who were a visible part of training programs and meetings.*—C.M.

Managers who are part of a learning organization have their role as coaches and champions laid out for them. The term "learning organization" is widely used, yet it is not to be taken lightly. To include managers as learning resources takes time and planning. The first focus on application occurs before the program is even designed. With proper positioning, you can require that managers be intimately involved in course design and development. You can use managers as sounding boards to help plan curricula.

Tanja Tuck, a consultant with Hewitt Associates, an HR consulting firm, describes how one of the firm's consulting areas used its management resources to design, develop, and present a successful training initiative. As a niche within the compensation practice, the consulting area specializes in sales practices, and its employees are typically people with master's degrees in business administration, who enjoy doing statistical analysis of sales reports. Because of the specialized nature of its service, the group's managers felt a need to develop their own "boot camp," or training ground for new employees.

Conscious of both time and budget, they also wanted to link the learning directly to on-the-job projects that would involve learners immediately. Consequently, the training leads participants through hands-on issues, such as case studies, calls from actual clients who have volunteered to be a part of the training, analysis of client issues, and problem solving with available data. The managers own the training and use it constantly. Tuck (2000) notes, "The associates in that group are so engaged that they also have a much higher retention rate than other areas in the organization."

Andrea Davison-Roberts, an experienced instructional designer and trainer, cites an experience working with managers while she was designing training for the computer reservation arm of an airline. Managers believed that service training was needed to solve many customer service problems that were occurring. As a result of an extremely careful needs analysis, including shadowing workers, she discovered that the problem stemmed from glitches in the system application. Consequently, management involvement in follow-up became essential so that the workers did not feel blamed for the problems. Having managers involved in the process from the beginning helped give impetus to the final recommendations for changing the system.

It is important to get the big picture and to ask managers to clarify their agendas, not only at the beginning, but throughout the learning initiative. You can ask them how they would like to be involved in the follow-up, helping them to understand that they are instrumental throughout the project. Another idea is to present executive previews for managers that include not only the content of the new program but also specific requests for support. Volunteers in the management group can even help teach portions of the program, as the Hewitt Associates managers did, or simply be visible during the pilot or kickoff sessions.

CATCH THE WAVE

My firm teamed with another to present a huge employee development initiative for a medium-sized manufacturing company in the highly competitive telecommunications industry; it involved a two-year rollout of communication training for employees and coaching training for managers. The needs analysis was extensive. Directors from every department were interviewed; key employees were involved in focus groups; schedule and budget frameworks were presented to the executive committee on a regular basis. Banners proclaiming, "Catch the Wave," the theme of the program, were displayed in the cafeteria two weeks before the kickoff.

With all of the proper procedures in place, the training was set for success, and, happily, two years later, it was deemed an instrumental contributor to more productive teamwork. As one of the key players, I led many of the focus groups and presented many of the classes, but one thing stands out as I recall that project: the depth of management commitment.

The commitment was evident from the beginning. The director of human resources personally introduced every opening module with a planned, inspirational message, positioning the importance of the training to the success of the organization. The other vice presidents and directors attended each required session, participating with the assembly line workers. They participated in activities, led discussions, and listened. The message that managers sent by supporting training and teamwork could not be missed. They were truly there for the employees. I've never seen anything quite like it since. We've stayed in touch with some of the trainees and their managers who shared that the training improved communication with the assembly teams and some key management-employee relationships. The technical areas, such as engineering, especially noticed the positive effects of increased communication.—C.M.

Sometimes, lack of know-how inhibits managers' involvement. For example, perhaps they have never taken part in a needs analysis or a focus group. They also may lack skills in coaching and feedback that are essential to help learners apply insights on the job. In response to needs such as these, David Beard, manager of customer service at Britain's BT global, developed a training curriculum that comprises specific steps for including managers. He describes the management involvement as follows: "Managers are instructed in coaching, identification of learning points, and a feedback model that shows different perceptions of an individual. They are given a summary of their employees' skill profiles and trained in career management and job skill development, including coaching and feedback skills. Managers and training consultants develop individual training programs for employees, targeted to meet individual training needs" (Younger, 1993).

Managers are a natural resource to trainers, but trainers must respect the many demands on managers' time. When working with managers, it is important to double check and clarify information you receive. Busy managers can sometimes give you inaccurate information unknowingly. Allen Chodl, a 21-year veteran of the training industry, describes an early training experience that went askew due to misinformation. He was to train truck driver/service representatives on sales skills. Previously, they had operated only as service people, but their job was expanded to include obtaining new business. The managers told him, "They're dying for information."

Surprisingly, he was faced with a resentful class of truck drivers, angry that their service role was changing. They did not want to sell. Nothing in his preparation had cued him in to their real feelings. Consequently, 95 percent of them left the company because of the revamped job role. In retrospect, Allen realized that had he spent more time with the managers in the beginning, the initiative would have been completely different. What the truck drivers really needed was to understand their changing job role and how they could benefit from it.

A final consideration in using managers involves budgeting. They can be required to either help pay or to pay in full for programs out of their own departmental budgets. This tactic encourages them to be involved with training design and to ensure that the learners' insights transfer to the job. The organization can reward managers and their teams for meaningful follow-up activities. The organization is the last and most all-encompassing natural resource for helping learners apply their new knowledge to make a bottom-line difference.

THE ORGANIZATION AS A RESOURCE

In his writings on servant leadership, Robert Greenleaf (1991) describes the role of the organization: "The first order of business is to build a group of people who, under the influence of the institution, grow taller and become healthier, stronger, more autonomous." Indeed, the institution—the organization—is the ultimate learning resource. Though perhaps most difficult to plan, design, and deliver, the visible, organizational support of learning initiatives is most essential to their success. Happily, true learning organizations, such as 3M, Southwest Airlines, and Hewitt Associates, are growing in number. Also, they are finding more creative ways to help employees focus on how to apply their new skills and knowledge.

Hands-on methods are generally part of the organization's learning culture. For example, Whirlpool Corporation in Benton Harbor, Michigan, supports a training program called "Real Whirled," targeted at sales trainers. As a part of the program, new hires live together in a seven-bedroom home near the headquarters and work as a team using Whirlpool home appliances to bake, wash, cook, and clean. According to the national manager of training for sales and operations, Jackie Seib, "It seems like such a no-brainer, but we tend to get away from spending time with the consumer" (Balu, 1999). Whirlpool found a way to bring the sales trainers closer to the consumer and, at the same time, enable the trainers to apply their knowledge immediately.

Other organizations tie learning initiatives into the hiring, orientation, performance appraisal, and customer feedback processes. Training specialists at the University of Chicago Hospitals Academy focus on application every time they identify a new employee competency to be developed. Judy Schueler, director of the Academy, describes how the learning strategy works: "Before we even start to design the curricula, we have to think about how we will ready the environment so that transfer of knowledge is possible. Organizations get discouraged by insufficient measurable outcomes because the environment hasn't been readied. We consider how it will impact the hiring processes. Will we be hiring differently as a result? For example, for our cultural diversity competency requirement, in the hiring process, candidates are asked questions such as, 'What has your past experience been working in a diverse work environment?' or 'What was your involvement?' and 'How have you built on that experience?'

"We then look at how our employee orientation program will be affected," Schueler continues. "Next, we discuss how are we going to appraise performance. Finally, if it's important enough to hold people accountable for, then it's important enough to ask our patients about. We ask a lot of questions in focus groups. We also have an array of employee recognition and award processes that recognize excellence in the particular competency. For example, with cultural competence, an employee who is appraised highly on the job in that area may also be eligible for a corresponding recognition award. A nurse who volunteers her time in the community tutoring disadvantaged children may apply for up to $1,000 to help that cause. These recognition programs, called employee foundation grants, are then given in that person's name" (Schueler, 2000).

The Academy's learning strategy has decreased the turnover rate by a full 10 percent, even in an unfavorable job market. The Academy uses the same strategy for such competencies as orientation to service, stewardship, and teamwork. During the planning phase, training and organization specialists use a grid that presents the plan of action. The learning strategy is not complete until all parts of the grid have been discussed.

Interestingly, the more organizations link training initiatives to career initiatives, the more they are encouraging self-managed employees. Employees can be required to demonstrate how they use new knowledge in their jobs. Such reports and demonstrations can be reinforced with positive articles in newsletters, on intranet bulletin boards, and in performance appraisals. Special rewards and recognition also reinforce application of learning. Executives who model how they have used new knowledge encourage the rest of the organization to do the same. As trainers, you can build organizational supports such as these into the planning and design of every training event you lead.

After all, the ultimate goal of most training initiatives is having happy, productive employees who are confident that their jobs have meaning for themselves, their managers, and their organizations. To build this confidence, Fox, Byrne, and Rouault (1999) suggest that organizations encourage mobility, provide employees with honest feedback, share key information, and support mentoring programs. They also suggest that organizations "inspire individuals to explore ways to connect what they really want to do with what the organization wants done . . . The goal is for people to feel that some part of their jobs provides value in a way that they find rewarding and satisfying."

THE BOTTOM-LINE DIFFERENCE

The ultimate test for any trainer is how effectively learners apply their new insights back at the workplace. By showing learners how to wisely use the most readily available natural resources—the individual, the manager, and the organization—you can lead them out of the classroom to be efficient and effective on the job. Judge how effectively you help the learners apply their insights with self-assessment 10-1.

Self-Assessment 10-1.
Are you focusing on application?

Directions: As you plan your next learning event, ask yourself if you have used your natural resources wisely. Consider these questions.

The Individual as Resource	The Manager as Resource	The Organization as Resource
• Have I encouraged individuals to focus on action planning?	• Have managers been involved from the beginning?	• Have I worked with others in the organization to incorporate a learning culture?
• Do I have inspirational questions and tools to stimulate future planning?	• Have I taken the time to get good, accurate information from managers?	• Do I understand what will happen to employees when they leave the classroom? How will they be supported?
• Did I incorporate simple, easy-to-use reminders of the importance of the skills and knowledge learned?	• Have I involved managers in the training itself?	• Can I contribute to communication tools, such as newsletters, presentations, bulletin board, intranet, etc., to recognize learners?
• Did I take into account the job roles of the participants and how the skills and knowledge will aid their career growth?	• Have I given managers some ideas for follow-up in their meetings and one-on-one conversations with employees?	• Do I understand how skills and knowledge are appraised, rewarded, and recognized by the rest of the organization?
• Did I suggest or require learners to present or share their knowledge with others?	• Have I suggested ways that they can reward and recognize employees for their training investment?	• Am I prepared to give feedback to other important leaders in the organization about the meaning of the training I lead?
	• Have I educated managers as to the coaching training available to them?	
	• Do managers know how the rest of the organization supports learning?	

11

ENCOURAGE COMMITMENT

In the preceding chapter, you explored how the individual, the manager, and the organization encourage application of knowledge. As the learning leader, how can you build application of knowledge into your training design? It all begins with commitment.

Personal commitment lies at the heart of all learning. After all, learning begins with one person's willingness to commit to his or her personal or professional growth. One person says, "I need to improve my technical skills," and signs up for a computer software course. Another individual recognizes that she needs to improve her managerial skills and enrolls in a leadership course. A third person gets feedback from his manager that he needs to improve his verbal communication and signs up for a presentation skills course. All these examples point to the fact that commitment is fundamental to learning.

COMMITMENT DEFINED

Because commitment is central to learning, you need to know how it is defined. A commitment has two interwoven sides: one action-oriented and the other feeling-oriented. Both aspects are present whenever commitments are made and kept. The first part of the definition states that a commitment is *a pledge or promise to do something in the future.* This is the actionable part of commitment. When you promise that you will take action, that is a commitment. Commitment also has an affective or feeling dimension. Commitment is also *a state of being obligated or emotionally impelled.* When you make a commitment to someone or to some group, you are pulled emotionally to make the commitment and to keep it. For example, when two people take part in a marriage ceremony, they are driven toward the goal because they love each other. They declare vows or promises to cement their commitment to each other in front of family and friends.

The same commitment dimensions apply in learning circumstances. When a person enrolls in a class and says, "I'm committed to improving my presentation skills," that individual has declared or pledged to improve. The person is emotionally propelled toward that goal because he or she perceives benefits from enhancing public speaking competencies. In every situation, whether a wedding or a class, the strength of a person's commitment varies from person to person and from situation to situation.

CRITICAL CONDITIONS

What conditions encourage commitment making and keeping? Kouzes and Posner (1987) point to three. First, people making commitments experience a sense of choice about their decisions. Commitment differs from compliance in this important aspect: People are free to commit or not to commit to a course of action. In the examples above, participants were free to attend or not to attend classes, and the couple was free to marry or not. Second, people are more likely to keep their commitments if they are visible to others. Marriage, with its public ceremony, is a good example of commitment visibility. Third, commitments are stronger when they are difficult to back out of or revoke. In other words, some form of accountability also helps people keep their commitments. This is the opposite of New Year's resolutions. Usually there is no accountability built into these well-meaning annual declarations. People make promises at some New Year's party and then forget them the next day.

Think of a time you made and kept a commitment. What circumstances encouraged you to declare the commitment and maintain it? Suppose you made a commitment to stop smoking. You made a pledge to yourself, your friends, and your spouse that you would begin on a certain date. You were emotionally drawn to this action by its health benefits and by your persistent cough. You had a clear choice—no one forced you to do it—although your spouse and friends encouraged you to stop your unhealthy habit. You kept your commitment visible by asking your spouse to keep a vigilant eye on you—to be certain you would not slip up and sneak a cigarette. Also, you joined a support group, which kept your commitment visible. Reporting to your support group also made it more difficult for you to renege on your promise. If you slipped up, your "smoking-cessation" team of friends, spouse, and support group members helped you get back on track. You created a network of support that kept your commitment to stop smoking both visible and difficult to revoke.

Commitments are promises or pledges to take some action in the future. They are also emotionally linked to you at a personal level. Three conditions encourage people to make and keep commitments: choice, visibility, and built-in accountability. How can you apply these commitment principles and practices to the classroom?

KEEPING COMMITMENTS THROUGH CHOICE

Participants have choices about their own level of involvement before the training begins. Senge (1990) notes that " . . . embarking on any path of personal growth is a matter of choice. No one can be forced to develop his or her personal mastery." Participants may choose to engage fully or just to go through the motions when it comes to their participation level. There are ways, however, that you can encourage them to choose full involvement.

The first way is to contact them by email or telephone and point out the benefits of attending and participating fully in your program. Master trainer Dan Heck

(1997), who trains regularly for Motorola and Ford Motor Company, indicates two benefits from contact before the class: "First, it diffuses most negative anticipation that worries a lot of participants, especially if they know they will have to practice skills in front of others. Second, it gives the facilitator a chance to hear more precisely what each participant wants out of the sessions. This personalization increases the validity of the class and the subsequent commitment to apply the concepts."

Asking questions that tie the course topics to the learners' personal needs forges an emotional link to the material. Such questions may be asked orally or in writing. For example, written prework could include questions about ways learners plan to apply material following the class. Questions can also focus on the benefits to participants, establishing an emotional link to the subject matter. As an example, as part of written prework for a course on negotiation, you can ask what benefits they would receive if the learners became better negotiators. As they answer this question, the learners begin to recognize that full engagement is in their best professional interest. Perhaps one participant will conclude that she will get a bigger bonus by negotiating better deals after the program. Another may realize that if he becomes more assertive with coworkers that he can improve his interpersonal relations at work.

The overall goal of this initial contact is to help participants recognize the personal benefits of attending the class and to move them to take responsibility for their training outcomes. As Bennis (1989) states, ". . . Adults learn best when they take charge of their own learning." You promote ownership by asking questions that let participants reflect on the training in personal ways and by engaging them in the learning process before the class.

As explained earlier, the opening or launch segment of your training program is critical for several reasons, including establishing a creative climate for learning and clarifying your role as learning partner. It is also at this point that you can introduce the concept of making and keeping commitments as an integral part of your learning design.

During your opening comments, explain that you have woven a commitment process into the design of the course. Define what a commitment is and indicate that learners can choose whether to commit. Their first choice is whether or not to participate in the commitment-to-action design. Remember, commitment differs from compliance because it is not mandatory. Learners should be given the freedom to choose not to commit. As Waterman (1987) explains, ". . . It's necessary to give people a choice about whether or not they will commit . . . If someone cannot choose not to commit, he probably won't take responsibility for his actions." Most participants will choose to participate in the process. The few that decide not to participate should be treated just like your other learners throughout the class. They may have enough commitments on their platter; do not judge them negatively for making that choice.

During your introductory comments, explain that another choice learners have is what to commit to. They decide which skills to work on during the class and which skills to improve after they return to work. You and the other learning partners can assist by providing useful feedback during the program, but ultimately each person must decide areas to focus on improving. During this opening phase, you may ask people to share this information with the class and post it. A participant in a self-management class may indicate that she wants to discover ways to spend more time with her family. Another person in the same class may say that he wants to become better organized. Organizations by Design president Toni Hupp (1996) has participants ". . . share, group, and prioritize 'hot issues' that they want to work on in training" to encourage committed learning. These opening expectations provide a foundation or database for subsequent commitment decisions.

During the launch phase, you also create support partners. Explain that the purpose of these peer partnerships is to provide mutual support during and after the class. Learning partners are encouraged after class to stay in weekly contact to support each other in working toward their commitments. Contact might be during a brief coffee break or via email. One way to help these peer partnerships get off to a good start is to build a partnering exercise into the opening phase. Such an exercise assists peers in bonding. Avoid assigning partnerships in advance. Letting learners forge their own partnerships is another way to share control and stimulate ownership of the process.

BUILDING SUPPORT PARTNERSHIPS

Here is one way that I have used to foster peer partnerships between learners at the beginning of a training program. I provide the following directions to the learning team:

1. Please take a minute to select someone to be your support partner. Here are the pros and cons of selecting someone you already know versus taking a chance with someone you have just met: When partners know each other, they are very comfortable giving each other support, and they know each other's foibles. On the other hand, people who are friends can find it difficult to coach each other rigorously, fearing it might rupture their relationship. Support partners who do not know each other expand their networking—professionally or within their organization. It is sometimes safer to share information with someone whom you do not know very well. What if it turns out that you are not very compatible? Remember, you will be partners for only a few weeks, it's not a marriage commitment! If your partnership is viable, it may last longer. You decide for yourselves. Having the freedom to choose your own partners is an important part of a genuine commitment process. Remember that you and your support partner will be meeting after the class is over to provide encouragement to each other for keeping your commitments.

2. Now, please take 10 minutes to interview your partner. You will be introducing him or her to the rest of the class, using these interview topics: name, department, number of years with the organization, outside interests, and skills your partner wants to improve in this class. This skill improvement question is in your prework.

3. Now that everyone has interviewed his or her partner, will each pair please come up to the front of the class and introduce each other to all of

us? I will record on the flipchart the item of skill improvement for each person. This will help me focus on what you want to get out of the class.

As each pair comes forward, I urge the class to applaud. This adds some levity to the activity. The challenge of coming in front of the class, a stressful experience for some participants, helps the pairs bond and sends the message that I will be sharing the spotlight throughout the learning event.—B.L.

Using peers has several advantages. A peer is *one who is of equal standing with another.* Because of this equal standing, status is removed as a potential communication barrier. Peers often feel free to share concerns and communicate openly since they enjoy equal status. As Finnerty (1996) notes, "Working with peers, people do not hesitate to ask for help for fear of appearing ignorant or having too small a problem to trouble a manager." Managers can provide good support too, but peers are often better suited.

PEERS TO THE RESCUE

From the beginning of the training session, I sensed something was wrong. Ken seemed quieter than usual. Normally, he was outgoing and talkative with a quick wit. He was about to go on vacation, shouldn't he be happier?

Ken had been placed in a new supervisory position with little or no training. A reorganization had thrust him into the job. At first, he got along fairly well. Now he was having real difficulty coping. Customers were complaining; his staff was in disarray. Ken was a self-reliant person. I wondered: Would he let his peers provide support?

As we completed our monthly brag session, Ken was hard-pressed to share a success story. When we moved on to the problem-solving segment of our monthly forum, everyone urged Ken to share his problem. Finally, after a good deal of gentle but persistent nudging from his fellow supervisors, Ken told them he was probably going to resign after his vacation. For an hour the group listened and offered support. Reluctantly, he swallowed his pride and accepted help. One person offered to train him in the skills he needed; another offered to lend him staff to get him over the hump.

Today, Ken likes to remind the vice president of his division how his peers saved his job. Ken is doing very well now. He's been promoted, but he almost lost his job and perhaps his career. His peers—not a mentor nor his manager—saved him. Peer power works. —B.L.

So far, the learners have made three choices. Before the class began, you encouraged them, through prework or personal contact, to choose involvement in their own learning. During the opening segment of the class, you explained that they would be able to participate or not participate in a commitment-to-action learning process. And, you gave them the choice of whom to select as their peer partner.

The most important choice is made at the end of each module. That is when each participant is given an opportunity to make preliminary commitments. These preliminary commitments enable learners to capture and record their insights

from the training segment that they have just completed. Since these are preliminary commitments, they enable the learners to try a commitment on for size. Final
commitments are made at the conclusion of the learning event, assuming that it
lasts one or more days. At that time, the learners can look over the preliminary
commitments and decide which ones to make final.

A preliminary commitment form (figure 11-1) allows participants to capture
insights and think of applications for the subject matter just completed. It
includes what the participant plans to do, who will be in his or her support network, and the potential risks and benefits associated with the planned action. A
preliminary commitment form usually appears at the end of a section in the learner's manual.

MAKE COMMITMENTS VISIBLE

Once commitments are chosen, they should be visible. How? After completing the
preliminary commitment form, the learning leader asks each participant to stand
up and declare his or her preliminary commitment to the learning team. This
makes the declaration public and visible. Taking a public stand can be intimidating for some, but it is an important aspect of the process. Public declarations help
enroll people in their own commitments and build team accountability. One participant stated when asked to declare her commitment, "I think I'm setting myself
up for failure by doing this." The learning leader responded, "Yes, and, you are
also setting yourself up for success!"

It is important for you to mention a few guidelines when you ask people to
declare their preliminary commitments to the group. First, if people wish to keep
their commitments confidential, you can allow that. Some learners may be making declarations that relate to a co-worker or their manager. In such cases, confi-

Figure 11-1. Example of a preliminary commitment form.

Preliminary Commitment
What action do you plan to commit to?

Who will you enlist to serve as your network of support?

When is your personal deadline for taking this action?

What are the potential risks of the action to which you are committing?

What are the potential benefits of the action to which you are committing?

dentiality is perfectly logical. They may also opt to keep a portion of their commitment confidential. For example, a participant could say, "I am going to meet with 'Mr. Jones' (a fictitious person) within the next three weeks to begin to resolve our conflict."

Second, coach people to make commitments that avoid using modifiers or conditional phrases. Lead-in words, such as "I hope to . . ." or "I may find time to . . ." signify less-than-full commitment. Instead, gently encourage participants to use assertive, definitive openings, such as "I will . . ." or "I promise to . . ." Even when preliminary commitments are spoken, it is important to keep the declarations positive. Hearing and sensing the full import of their commitment helps the learners decide whether their preliminary commitments should be put in final form later on.

Final commitments are written and declared at the end of the program. As participants complete commitment-to-action forms, they huddle with their peer partners to decide when to meet. Do not rush this process. Allow at least 20 minutes at the end of your program for these important planning steps.

Figure 11-2 is an example commitment-to-action form that you may integrate into your training materials for the learners. It is normally positioned as the final page of a manual. Commitments should remain visible so that participants are reminded of them daily. Some participants may wish to create visible reminders on monitor screen savers, index cards, or their daily planners.

BUILD IN ACCOUNTABILITY

In addition to providing for choice and making commitments visible, the third critical element is building in accountability. Peer partnering helps with accountability. As peer partners meet weekly, they become responsible to each other for results. Often these meetings are very brief, perhaps short encounters over coffee. Other meetings can be longer, for example, coaching and rehearsing each other as part of a presentation skills program. No matter how brief or long the meetings are, their purpose remains the same: to provide mutual support to attain commitment. Peer partners, however, need a way to report on each other's progress.

A follow-up session is critical for real accountability. Such a commitment reporting session may be designed as part of the training modules. The first portion of the second module may be devoted to reporting on work accomplished between the first and second sessions and so on. Normally, these commitment reporting and learning exchanges, during which participants learn from each other as they discuss their trials and errors, last about 45 minutes to an hour, depending on your class size. When peer partners know they will be reporting on their partners' progress, more application of knowledge occurs. It is just human nature for participants to work harder if they know that they will be reporting on their progress to a learning team. How is such a follow-up session conducted?

After welcoming all the learners back, take time to establish a framework for open dialogue by talking abo .ut the success or failure of a commitment. Remind them that commitment progress shouldn't be judged by measurable results alone. Progress is also evident when people learn from trial and error.

Figure 11-2. Example of a commitment-to-action form.

Commitment to Action

Name:_____ Date: _____

I hereby commit to this action:	My deadline for taking this action is (date):

Besides my support partner, my support network will include the following people:

Name: _____

Name: _____

Name: _____

The potential benefits from working toward my commitments are:

Commitment	Benefit

I will keep my commitments *visible* by:

_____

_____

_____

My support partner is:_____.

His or her telephone number: _____ **Fax:** _____

Email:_____.

My support partner will speak with me on :_____(date)
at_____(time).

For example, one manager, who had made a commitment to listen to her staff by giving them her full attention, discovered that she needed to move from behind her desk to a round table in her office. This slight change in physical setting allowed her to concentrate better on what people were saying. Before that realization, she was distracted by items on her desk or by her computer's email function. When she shared this insight with the learning team, several others chimed in that they would change their listening space, too. This is a small example of the kind of learning that happens when participants share knowledge. This seemingly trivial behavioral change made a big difference when it came to the manager's relationship with her staff. Others at the commitment reporting session benefited, too. To get your participants to open up and share such commitment success stories requires keen listening and facilitation skills.

After talking about commitment success and failure, here are the steps you could take to facilitate a commitment reporting session:

1. Ask the peer partners to meet together for three to five minutes to get last-minute progress reports from each other. Remind them that each of them will report on the other's commitment progress in a few minutes.
2. Go around the table and ask each partner to report on the other's commitment progress.
3. Before moving to the next pair, ask each participant to elaborate on his or her own commitment progress. Facilitate this by asking great questions, such as: "Tell us how you accomplished that . . ." or "What methods did you use that worked for you?" or "What did you learn by working on that commitment?" or "Please share any additional insights . . . ." Such follow-up questioning is very useful, because the participants are celebrating their successes, sharing their insights with the learning team, as well as helping each other overcome any barriers encountered as they worked on their commitments. This probing is at the heart of the learning exchange.
4. Then, remind the participants about making new commitments (or carrying old ones forward) at the end of this session. They should write them out, huddle with their partners to decide on times to meet, and declare their commitments to the learning team at the end of the session.
5. Finally, be sure to acknowledge and congratulate the team on the commitment progress they made together. Point out that learning was generated by them during this reporting phase of their training.

COMMITMENT SUCCESS STORIES

As you fold the commitment process into your training design, you may wonder what kinds of commitments learners make and the results they achieve. Success stories reveal the potential power of commitment design. Not everyone in your classes will make such progress, but many will if you provide the opening and a framework for such committed action. Following is a sampling of results you may expect based on real stories of commitment progress:

*   A young, professional woman in Houston makes a commitment to study for her certified public accountant (CPA) exam after work, instead of leaving the office at 5 p.m. and fighting rush-hour traffic. The result? She passes the examination on the first try. Her support partner encourages her to stay each evening, even while he is on vacation! He accomplishes this feat by programming his computer to send her computer a friendly reminder message each day when she boots up her computer: "Are you planning to stay tonight to study?" This is an interesting example of a personal approach facilitated by high technology.
*   Two professionals at a national association support each other after a presentation skills program. They rehearse each other before speaking engagements, focusing on specific skills they want to improve. The result? They both make progress in such skill areas as eye contact with listeners and a slower delivery pace. Both partners also attend each other's presentations and then provide useful feedback afterward. They report on their commit-

ment progress during session two, about 30 days after the initial session, with the facilitator encouraging them to elaborate on how they provided this excellent support to each other.

HOW DO YOU ENCOURAGE LEARNERS TO MAKE COMMITMENTS?

Commitment is fundamental to learning. When learners make a commitment, they are propelled toward their goals. They are expressing their willingness in the form of a promise to carry their insights back to the job, where it will make a difference to the organization. How effectively do your training offerings encourage learners to make and keep commitments? Self-assessment 11-1 is a checklist to help you assess skills that help learners make commitments to learning and applying their insights.

Self-Assessment 11-1. Commitment design checklist.

Directions: Use this checklist to help you integrate personal commitment into your training designs. Place a check in the appropriate column when you have completed the design element listed.

Design Element	Yes	No
I help participants become committed to their own learning and development through prework questions or preclass contact.		
I introduce the commitment process during the opening phase of my training programs.		
I provide participants choices regarding the commitment process: whether to participate, who their support partner will be, which areas they wish to improve.		
I give participants an opportunity to capture and try out commitments by including preliminary commitments at the end of every major section of my program.		
I use peer partnerships to provide follow-up support.		
I design commitment-to-action forms for participants to write down their commitments and spell out times that they will meet with their support partners before the follow-up session.		
I encourage commitment visibility by having participants stand and declare their commitments to the learning team.		
I coach participants to use positive, unqualified language when they declare their commitments.		
I schedule commitment reporting and learning exchange sessions for peer partners to report their progress, celebrate success, and share insights with the learning team.		
I use skillful team facilitation skills to probe for wisdom as participants report on their commitments.		

12

COACH FOR
RESULTS

Leading the learner means not only leading in team settings, it also includes leading during one-on-one coaching situations. Individualized, one-on-one coaching is a natural extension of team coaching. As you facilitate a team of learners, you often develop a close bond or rapport with participants. This trusting relationship may naturally progress into a coaching role for the trainer. Because you may coach a key executive or manager, the success of your coaching can have a tremendous effect on both the person being coached and the person's organization. Coaching saves managers' jobs by helping them improve career-dependent skills, provides for clearer communication within a work team, and enables executives to make thoughtful decisions.

Coaching partnerships may also grow out of informal conversations. A participant sends an email or calls you with a question: "How should I handle getting approval from my manager for this new project? He seems closed to my suggestions." Perhaps you run into a vice president in the hall who asks you to step into her office for a brief chat about one of her staff: "John appears to be losing interest in his role as customer service manager. How do you think I should approach him at our weekly meeting?" In each of these examples, your first instinct is to provide an answer, because that would be the most efficient and timely approach. Is it, however, the best way to lead the learner toward self-sufficiency? Maybe it is not.

COACH DEFINED

Before exploring the best approach to coaching you should be clear about what it means. Coaching has many definitions and interpretations. Finnerty (1996), in *The ASTD Training & Development Handbook,* explains its broad scope: "Coaching in the narrowest sense is the process of helping a single employee improve a particular aspect of his or her performance. In the broadest sense it is the management role associated with high-performance teams." Peters and Austin (1985) say, "Coaching is the process of enabling others to act, of building on their strengths." These definitions apply primarily to a manager who is doing on-the-job coaching.

In a training context, a coach is *someone who aids, assists, or empowers another person to take appropriate action.* Coaching is used in this chapter to mean a one-on-one, private session or series of sessions, between a participant and a learning leader.

BENEFITS OF COACHING

More managers and executives are turning to executive or professional development coaching for several reasons. Caudron (1996) points out that ". . . the entrepreneurial movement has dramatically increased the number of people working at home without an organizational support system. Through regular contact, coaches provide the kind of personalized feedback and motivation formerly provided by bosses and co-workers. Even individuals who remain in corporate America find coaches a valuable resource because downsizing has eliminated many of the managers and mentors they used to turn to for support."

Whatever the specific reason, Morris (2000) observes, "Coaches are everywhere these days . . . Workers at all levels of the corporate ladder, fed up with a lack of advice from inside the company, are taking matters into their own hands and enlisting coaches for guidance on how to improve their performance, boost their profits, and make better decisions about everything from personnel to strategy." An executive or professional development coach also provides these additional benefits:

- targeted, individualized learning
- flexible scheduling of coaching sessions
- an objective point of view
- a safe and confidential outlet to vent and solve problems.

Unlike traditional classroom training, one-on-one coaching allows the coach and learner to focus on issues that the learner is facing. It is just-in-time, personal attention.

Busy executives and managers appreciate the customized scheduling that this kind of coaching permits. Usually conducted in one- to three-hour chunks, professional development coaching may be scheduled to suit the hectic timeframe of your client. You also have the flexibility of conducting the sessions at the manager's location or at another facility. Often the confidential nature of these sessions dictates the location. Depending on the person's needs, coaching may last from one session to six sessions, sometimes spread out over a four- to six-month period.

Since bosses and peers are often too close to the parent organization to offer objective advice, an outside coach can often be more objective. This is true whether the coach is an in-house trainer or an outside consultant.

Coaching offers the learner another major benefit: a safe haven for discussing, exploring, and making decisions about important work-related issues. Many successful executives, who are not facing any particular crisis or skill deficit, turn to coaches for introspection and reflection. The ability to step back, pause, and ponder issues is a valuable natural resource.

QUALITIES OF A GREAT COACH

These benefits do not happen automatically, however. To be an effective coach, you must possess certain innate qualities. A great deal of power resides in a coach. A successful coaching assignment can have a profound effect on a person's career, for example. To discover the natural qualities that most great coaches have, think about an effective coach you have worked with in the past. Perhaps this person was an athletic coach, musical coach, or another trainer. Then, complete self-assessment 12-1. No matter which qualities you circled on the self-assessment, a foundation of authentic service and integrity must underscore all successful coaching. Then, three skills come into play: attending to the person, asking questions and listening, and agreeing on action.

ATTENDING TO THE PERSON

Attending to the person involves being certain he or she is ready for one-on-one coaching. You discover in advance, through a brief telephone or in person conversation, why the person is considering coaching. Is it to satisfy his or her manager, or is it because the person is sincere about developing professionally? If the person's motive is genuine, the coaching is more likely to succeed. If the person's motive is to look good for someone else, you may decide to decline that coaching assignment. Once the person has "qualified" for coaching, you attend by being certain the physical environment is free from distractions, comfortable, and equipped with a flipchart and marker as tools.

Giving your full attention means more than the physical setup. By attending to the person, you are focusing on his or her needs. To do that you build a trust-

---

Self-Assessment 12-1.
Do you have what it takes to be a great coach?

Directions: Think of someone in your experience who was a great coach—a teacher, music instructor, athletic coach, a trainer, or perhaps a religious leader. Circle the words that best describe that person. Note patterns and connections as you complete this activity. Then, check the top three qualities. Which of these qualities do you demonstrate?

helpful	direct	subtle	tough	understanding
honest	forthright	listener	competent	closed
patient	friendly	open	talkative	pushy
nice	demanding	clear	questioning	personal
negotiator	warm	motivator	cold	knowledgeable
observer	egotistical	interested	dominating	fair
respectful	energetic	expecting	partner	controlling
critical	confident	assisting	tricky	other:
positive	nervous	smooth		

ing, open, and friendly partnership. You reveal your own methods, shortcomings, and limitations. For example, you tell the participant during a stretch coaching session that you may interrupt him or her as a new skill is practiced. You explain that the reason for the interruption is to enable the person to try a different approach, just as a choir director asks singers to repeat a musical phrase using a different pitch or tempo. You also give the person permission to let you know if you are pushing too hard, thereby giving permission for the person to push back. If you use commitment making as part of a coaching process, you explain how it works and why you use it. Being transparent about your methods builds trust and partnership.

Attending also means being present and giving your full attention to the person you are coaching and to what is going on at that moment. You empty your mind—in the Zen sense—of distracting thoughts and judgments. NBA coach Phil Jackson describes this Zen emphasis on clearing the mind: "What pollutes the mind in the Buddhist view is our desire to get life to conform to our peculiar notion of how things *should* be, as opposed to how they really are" (Jackson & Delehanty, 1995). When you clear your mind of self-centered thoughts, such as "Look at the great job I'm doing!" or "I wonder how this will turn out?" you are able to focus on what is happening now. You are able to center on supporting the person you are coaching without worrying about the ultimate outcome too much. Being in the present is a gift you create for yourself and the person you are supporting.

When you clear your mind, it enables the person being coached to focus, too. Corporate coach Linda Impastato (1999) puts it this way: "The true gift of a good coach is to create a space where individuals can clearly think about what *they* want to get done, not what I expect from them." Asking a great question, such as, "What do you want to work on today?" can help create that spacious meadow for learning.

ASKING QUESTIONS AND LISTENING

Skillful coaching always includes asking great questions. Moving beyond technique, it is important for the coach to reflect on the reason he or she is asking a question. Are you asking the question to assist the person in discovering his or her own answers? If so, you are making an assumption that the person is capable and wise. When you ask questions in this context, it helps you avoid treating the person being coached as needy, dependent, or weak.

A coach often gets the best results by providing a space for the person to listen to themselves, reflect quietly, and come up with an answer or approach that works for that individual. Turning again to NBA basketball coach Phil Jackson, it is clear he knows how to use powerful listening to get great results from his players. "I find that when I can be truly present with impartial, open awareness, I get a much better feel for the players' concerns than when I try to impose my own agenda," he says. "And, paradoxically, when I back off and just listen, I get much better results on the court" (Jackson & Delehanty, 1995). Learning leaders can use the same approach to good effect during coaching sessions.

PAUSE POWER

I was giving a talk on empowerment coaching to a professional group of trainers when I discovered the power of pausing. As part of the program I coached a volunteer, Bill, from the audience. About 60 people observed us. At one point I asked Bill, "Is there anything else about this issue that you want to share?" Bill was silent. I had a feeling that he wanted to say more. Bill had a very thoughtful look on his face, so I gave him some time to think. He reflected for about a minute. Remember, 60 people were observing. You could have heard a pin drop in the room. Finally, Bill said, "Yes. I want to tell you about a time that I had this terrible experience with a co-worker." He went on to talk about this bad relationship with a co-worker; the experience had been keeping him from trusting others at work as his career developed. By allowing Bill to take his time to communicate, he was able to recall an important event in his life. Later, when we debriefed in front of the audience, Bill said that by giving him the extra minute or so of silence to think, he was able to share an important barrier to relating to others. This "eureka" insight led to a new commitment: Bill agreed to begin trusting co-workers more and to begin that process by scheduling lunches with two peers within the next month. Pausing has great power. —B.L.

AGREEING ON ACTION

The ultimate objective of all coaching approaches is to get the person to change his or her behavior, whether it is a narrow skill or a broad attitude. That is why it is always important to include an application or commitment segment to your coaching. Getting final agreement on the desired outcome is an integral step.

Agreeing on action occurs throughout the coaching process. At the beginning, agreement is reached on subjects, methods, and timeframe. Agreement on coaching objectives is achieved by asking the person to develop a list of objectives before the first coaching session. You recommend that the person obtain feedback from his or her manager, peers, and clients on their strengths and weaknesses. Often, the individual has gone through a formal assessment process, such as 360-feedback (when feedback comes from the manager, peers, and subordinates) or assessments conducted at personal development seminars. In addition, performance appraisals offer useful insights. All this data may be used to help the person focus on issues for coaching. As you conduct coaching sessions, ask for feedback to make sure you are still in agreement about these issues. You may ask, "Are we still focused on the right topics?" or "Are we still in agreement about my role?" or "Are we still in agreement about how you apply insights from our coaching sessions to real-life situations back at work?" At the conclusion of a coaching session you reach agreement with the learner on what action she or he wants to take back at work. Because you have agreed at the beginning that your sessions include an application process, you do not have to push for committed action. You have also agreed to review the learner's commitment progress at the beginning of your next coaching session. As discussed in chaper 11 on commitment, the elements of choice, visibility, and accountability are all built into the coaching design. The learner agrees on what to focus on during the coaching sessions and what to commit to between coaching sessions. So choice is an integral element for ownership. You assist the learner to design ways to keep their coaching commitments visible at work. An index card posted near a desk, a screen saver message on a computer, or a note in a daily planner—all serve to keep commitments visible. The third commitment element, accountability, is accomplished by having the person report on his or her progress at the next session.

TWO TYPES OF COACHING

As a learning leader you are called upon to coach in two specific ways: stretch coaching and empowerment coaching. During a particular coaching assignment, you may use one or both approaches. Stretch coaching is used whenever someone is trying to improve a specific skill. You use stretch coaching to encourage the individual to expand his or her repertoire of skills. In so doing, you often stretch the person to move outside his or her comfort zone. For example, you can help someone improve his or her verbal presentation skills during a one-on-one coaching session. As this person practices certain skills, such as voice projection or pausing between phrases, you would use stretch coaching. Sometimes, the use of an audio recorder or videocamera and playback system is appropriate for stretch coaching, because these technologies allow the learner to observe and modify the approach used.

The second type of coaching is empowerment coaching. Empowerment coaching comes into play when a person comes to you with a problem or issue. Instead of providing the answer, you use the empowerment coaching model to enable the person to craft an answer. Now, you are ready to apply the principles of coaching—attending to the person, asking questions and listening, and agreeing on action—to stretch coaching.

STRETCH COACHING

As mentioned earlier, stretch coaching helps the learner improve a specific skill. You may be called upon, for example, to coach someone about how to interview a job applicant. You have provided a six-step interview model. The first step of the model is "Greet applicant and establish rapport." Here is the way you could apply stretch coaching to this interview model.

- *Agree on a coaching objective.* You and the learner have agreed that he wants to enhance his interviewing skills.
- *Explain the coach's role and methods.* You explain that as the learner role-plays this first step in the interview process, you may interrupt and ask the learner to modify the approach. You apologize for the way this method may interrupt the learner's train of thought, explaining that in your experience this is still the best way to coach for skill improvement; that is, immediate, specific feedback provides the best results. You also mention that you may be stretching the learner outside the comfort zone, because this may be an unfamiliar approach.

- *Model the skill by using the "what and why" approach.* You demonstrate the proper way to welcome an applicant: going to greet him as he waits in the lobby, conversing in a friendly tone, showing interest in him as a person, and revealing some things about yourself to establish rapport. You use a "what and why" approach as you model. That is, you show the learner what to do and tell him why it is important. In this first step of the interview model, for example, you demonstrate ways to establish rapport. You tell the learner that these opening conversations are important, because the success or failure of the interview may depend on the trust that is established early.
- *Ask the learner to demonstrate the skill.* Have the learner practice the skill. Assure him that this is merely practice and that perfection is not expected.
- *Interrupt and coach to the model.* As the learner practices the interview model, gently interrupt to provide useful feedback. You may say, "Bill, please slow down a bit. You seem to be rushing this conversation a little. Remember that you are trying to put the applicant at ease with small talk. Going too fast may make him nervous. Please go back and try that again. Thanks."
- *Acknowledge progress.* When the learner has demonstrated proficiency on the skill, offer congratulations. Also, thank him for being "coachable" during the practice session.
- *Encourage application of the new skill.* Offer a forum for the learner to make a commitment to apply the new skill during the next job interview. Build in a follow-up session to assess on-the-job application of the skill after the learner has had an opportunity to use it in the real world.

When applied with flexibility and patience, stretch coaching can yield dramatic results for a specific skill in a very short period of time. One key is to use your behavioral model flexibly, integrating it with the natural style of the person being coached. Being too rigid in applying your model is a sure way to discourage the person you are coaching, build resistance to your ideas, and block any hope of on-the-job application.

THE INTERRUPTER

I once coached a woman for listening skill improvement. Her inability to listen was keeping her not only from being effective, but also from moving up in her area within a large, commodity-trading organization. Because the work environment was so volatile, noisy, and loud, her poor skills went unnoticed until she was put in charge of a special project and had to work with other departments more frequently and more quietly. During the coaching process, we determined that interrupting was her most frequent bad habit, and we began to role-play typical work conversations to see if she could catch herself. In subsequent discussions, however, she was unable to determine whether or not she was interrupting. Finally, I audiotaped our conversation and, during its playback, she realized how many times she had interrupted me. She shared that she had probably inherited the habit from her mother, who was a consistent interrupter, even during their adult conversations. This experience solidified for me that, with a little time and attention, coaching can often uncover long-unnoticed habits.—C.M.

EMPOWERMENT COACHING

Empowerment coaching is used for different situations. It is used whenever someone requests assistance with a problem, a professional development objective, or a career advancement issue. The main objective of this coaching is to encourage the learner to find his or her own answers. In other words, it is a self-discovery process. It also empowers the learner to act.

Empowerment coaching is helpful at the beginning stages of executive coaching. It helps clarify what the person wants to achieve. Here is an example of how it can be applied during an executive coaching session: You are conducting your first session with an executive who wants to work on improving her networking skills. You would use the four-step empowerment coaching model to explore this improvement area and begin to generate possible actions for her to take. The dialogue may go something like this:

1. Select a topic for coaching.

    Coach: "Mary, we have agreed to work on three areas during our work together. Which issue would you like to begin working on?"

    Mary: "Let's begin with networking. My manager listed that as my number-one area for improvement on my last performance appraisal, and I agree with her. I hate to go outside my area and talk with other managers!"

    Coach: "Okay. That sounds like a good place to begin."

2. Determine why it is important to the person.

    Coach: "Mary, let me find out why this issue is so important to you. As you answer, I'm going to jot down your responses on this white board."

    Mary: "Well, let's see. It's important because I know I should do it."

    Coach: "Why should you do it?"

    Mary: "I should do it because I need to get to know my peers in other departments. If I became better acquainted with their operations, I might understand how my area affects theirs. I need to understand how my department works within the entire system."

    Coach: "That sounds logical. Are there any other reasons to get to know them?"

    Mary: "Let me think. If got to know them, perhaps we could support each other."

    Coach: "What do you mean?"

    Mary: "Well, sometimes I ask for assistance from my co-workers in other departments and they brush me off. If I got to know them better maybe I wouldn't get the cold shoulder so often. We might support each other better."

Coach: "All right. Good. Now, why is it important for you to get their support?"

Mary: "Because I'm under too much pressure and need someone to talk to."

Coach: "How would that help you?"

Mary: "I might get a good night's sleep and stop worrying so much! My doctor has told me I need to get more rest."

Coach: "So, networking with your peers might actually improve your sleep and overall health. Is that correct?"

Mary: "Yes."

Coach: "Very good Mary. So we've agreed that improving your networking skills is important to you. Let's recap to be sure I have understood all your reasons. Networking would improve your understanding of how your work affects other departments, create a network of support among your peers, enhance your health and well-being, improve your chances for promotion, and teach you the advantages of teamwork. Those are great insights, Mary! Now, let's talk about possible actions you could take to improve your networking."

3.   Explore what the person is willing to do about it.

Coach: "Mary, what have you thought about doing to improve your networking?"

Mary: "Well. I don't know. What do you think I should do?"

Coach: "Before I share my ideas, I would like to get your thoughts. Let's just brainstorm some possible actions you might take."

Mary: "Okay. Well, I could read a book on networking."

Coach: "Yes. I can recommend a book on that. I'll give you the author and title before you leave today. What else?"

Mary: "I could meet with two of my co-workers and talk about work issues."

Coach: "That sounds like a good idea. What are their names?"

Mary: "Bill Thomas and Joan Steinberg."

Coach: "It helps to set a time limit for these actions: when could you meet with them?"

Mary: "Let's see—within the next two weeks."

Coach: "Great. Is there anything you need to do to prepare for your meetings?"

Mary: "Not really. They are two people I like already, so meeting with them won't be that difficult. After I meet with them, I may need some help with the other folks I should talk with."

Coach: "Okay. Well, let's summarize what you will be doing before our next meeting. You will meet with Bill and Joan during the next two weeks, and I will give the name of a book you can purchase on networking. When you return in three weeks for our next session, we'll discuss ideas from the book, and we'll talk how your meetings went with your co-workers."

Mary: "Good. I'm writing these actions down in my weekly planner so I won't forget."

4. Offer support.

Coach: "Mary, is there anything else I can do to help you?"

Mary: "Well . . . Is it okay if I call you after my first meeting and talk about how it went?"

Coach: "Of course. Here's my card with my number. I'm always available to chat between sessions. If I'm not there, leave a message on my voicemail. I'll try to get back within 24 hours."

Mary: "Thanks. This was a very good first session. I feel good about the fact that I'm beginning to work on my problems."

What you have done very skillfully in this scenario is use the person's wisdom to develop solutions. You have created a spacious meadow for her to play in, reflect, and decide on a course of action. The second step in the empowerment coaching model (discovering why the issue is important) provides the motivation for action. When Mary realizes what is at stake—her career, promotions, and even her health—she has developed a platform to stand on as she ponders networking actions. By using the four empowerment coaching steps and the general coaching skills of attending, asking great questions, and agreeing on action, you conducted a very successful coaching session.

BECOMING AN EFFECTIVE COACH

Coaching is a skill that every learning leader should master. Many of the same natural approaches used in the classroom—serving with integrity, asking great questions, and listening powerfully—apply to coaching, too. The learning partnerships you forge in the classroom often lead to one-on-one coaching assignments. Two types of coaching approaches occur: stretch coaching, when a specific skill is improved, and empowerment coaching, when a problem area is revealed and solutions discovered by the learner. In both types of coaching you use three *As*:

- *Attending* to the person's needs by being present and focused
- *Asking* questions and listening to help the person discover insights and actions
- *Agreeing* to move beyond talking to doing by having the person declare his or her intentions and report on progress throughout your coaching sessions.

By expanding your coaching talents to your clients, you become a more valuable asset to the organization or groups you serve. Self-assessment 12-2 can help remind you of critical coaching skills.

Self-Assessment 12-2.
Coaching checklist.

Directions: Please check the appropriate box to indicate your coaching strengths and improvement areas.

Coaching Skill	Yes	No	Needs Improvement
1. I look and listen for opportunities to provide one-on-one coaching.			
2. I assume the people I coach are wise, able, and self-sufficient.			
3. I recognize that my role is to aid and assist, not impress or save the person being coached.			
4. I realize that more and more managers and executives are turning to one-on-one coaching for their professional development.			
5. I respect the confidentiality of the person I am coaching.			
6. I provide a safe place for venting, reflecting, and solving problems.			
7. I offer an objective point of view for the person being coached.			
8. I individualize my approach for each person I coach.			
9. I offer flexible, just-in-time coaching.			
10. I give honest feedback to the person I am coaching.			
11. I "qualify" people before accepting coaching assignments.			
12. I set up the physical environment for comfort and privacy.			
13. I establish mutual expectations regarding topics and approach with the person being coached.			
14. I give my full attention to the person during coaching sessions.			
15. I ask great questions and listen keenly during coaching.			
16. I use silence and reflective listening to assist the person discover answers.			
17. I help the person I'm coaching agree on appropriate action back on the job.			
18. I use stretch coaching to help people improve specific skills.			
19. I use empowerment coaching to help people discover their own answers.			
20. I realize the responsibility I have to coach with integrity.			

13

FLEX FOR THE FUTURE

A re you sluggish and out of shape? As a trainer, are you bogged down in the status quo, enjoying a false sense of contentment while resting on your laurels? If your answer is yes, perhaps you need to start a workout program to flex for the future. Trainers who train from the heart are able to feel the pulse of the everchanging workplace. If you are in tune and truly flexed for the future, you are able to

- provide current or updated programs
- use appropriate technology for delivery and communication
- understand today's business climate
- respond to changing workforce demographics
- market and network nonstop
- consider reinventing your role.

Do you engage in future-focused training, or are you guilty of lack of knowledge or action? Perhaps you need to flex your training muscles a bit, with an eye to the future.

DO YOU PROVIDE CURRENT, UPDATED PROGRAMS?

How often have you pulled out a course module with the intent of announcing it on your company's training calendar, only to be embarrassed that it hasn't been revised in five to 10 years? Do you go ahead and offer it anyway, hoping that no one will notice? Sadly, this is often the case. Yet, adult learners have changed; they have new interests and new workplace challenges to meet. They are better informed than ever before, and they will be able to detect outdated material.

In the last decade, there has been additional research in every area in which you provide training. Are you being fair to employees if you are not including it? Stay up to date with both the content and design of your programs. Have you included new developments in the field? Does your team building program acknowledge the gradual shifts that teams in the workplace have made over the past decade? Does your leadership and communication training acknowledge the areas of emotional intelligence and intuition? Does your presentation skill training incorporate the use of computer-generated visuals? If you use a video in any of your programs, is it current? Do you keep your use of video, computer-based, Web-based, and interactive, in-person programming in balance?

Technology can help you stay updated in many ways. For example, with the ease of Internet research, it is not difficult to update program content. Updating may be as simple as exploring the Web for the latest articles on a certain topic or a more complex research to advance a theory. Excellent research sites like Electric Library (elibrary.com), Northern Light (northernlight.com) and Harvard Business Review (hbr.org/forum) can be accessed with a few clicks of the mouse.

Telecommunications technologies, such as email and voicemail, can also help you update programs. They can make it easier to obtain the interviews and information typically needed for content updates. As you learned in earlier chapters, getting information from your customers increases their commitment to the program. It also keeps you current and flexed for the future.

With respect to program design, the latest word-processing programs make editing a breeze. Even trainers with a rudimentary background in instructional design are able to navigate today's software programs. Computer graphics programs provide instant clipart, in addition to more sophisticated illustration tools. There is really no excuse any more for not providing learners with up-to-date material.

Finally, you can set a goal to be knowledgeable about current trends. Put a future focus on your own professional development. Read magazines, such as ASTD's *Training & Development,* Lakewood Publishing's *Training,* or any of the countless other journals and publications dedicated to HR management, employee development, management development, information technology, presentations, and sales training. ASTD's *Info-line* is a popular source for quick reviews on all the latest topics; over the years it has covered project management, distance learning, and training of senior workers, to name a few. Crisp Publications has a longstanding series of how-to books to keep you current on training topics. Most magazines and journals have Websites and chat rooms. You do not necessarily need another advanced degree to stay on top of trends.

DO YOU USE APPROPRIATE TECHNOLOGY FOR DELIVERY AND COMMUNICATION?

The 2000 ASTD State of the Industry Report showed that the use of the technology to deliver training increased 50 percent from 1996 to 1997, but that use of learning technologies actually *fell* during the period 1997–1998 (McMurrer, Van Buren & Woodwell, 2000). It could be that the combination of budgeting, designing, training, and implementing such technologies proved too challenging for organizations. Often, organizations adopt a "wait-and-see" philosophy when a change initiative is too cumbersome. Even if organizations encounter challenges implementing and budgeting technology-based training, the Web has certainly opened new horizons for those in the training profession.

Strauss (1999), writing on Web-based training, lists the major Internet technologies now in use: online computer-based training (CBT), online references, performance support systems, newsgroups, listserv discussions, chat sessions, virtual classrooms, email, and streaming audio and video. He explains that virtual classrooms extend the chatroom concept by simulating real classrooms online and using graphics, animation, and interactive activities.

Trainers are converting existing training materials that are available as word-processing documents into hypertext markup language (HTML) files so they can be viewed with a Web browser. Others are having their Webmaster install listserv software so that people can leave messages about training for others in cyberspace.

Telecommuting and videoconferencing will continue to replace many traditional face-to-face business settings; for example, Dallas-based Meetings Professionals International indicated that 49 percent of its corporate meeting planners expected to plan fewer gatherings in 2000 than they did in 1999 (Crain's Communications, 2000). These statistics reveal a corporate meeting trend that trainers should watch. For example, if your client's meetings are typically a training venue for you, your opportunity to coordinate with them may diminish in the future. You may need to find new ways to get information across to large departmental groups. Instead of providing training in break-out sessions at the annual sales meeting, you may need to plan computer-based conferencing, reading assignments, and chats to communicate new product knowledge. Meetings have also traditionally been the locale to encourage and motivate employees. How, as a trainer, will you suggest that managers build motivating climates outside of the corporate meeting environment? You may want to suggest smaller local retreats or events with a variety of facilitators to lead key discussions.

Karen Lawson, principal of Lawson Consulting Group and author of eight books on training, reveals how videoconferencing has already affected the way she delivers training. Recently, she presented a three-hour Train-the-Trainer program for approximately 140 trainers in a large financial services organization. Only 70 were with her in the classroom, however. The others were watching via videoconference from Florida and Colorado, and five were listening to a teleconference of the program. To make this event happen, Lawson had to make plans for preparing her fellow facilitators in Colorado and Florida, and she had to find ways to work around the unavoidable video signal delays. Distance formats are indeed challenging for those who create interactive training formats! A proponent of interactive learning, Lawson (2000) suggests that the Web and CD-ROM formats work best for ". . . getting cognitive information quickly," but she prefers face-to-face interaction for practicing communication and sales skills.

Another organization that has adapted to technology quickly and wisely is Philadelphia-based Brody Communications, owned by Marjorie Brody, a speaker, trainer, and author of 15 books on business communication and etiquette. The Brody Communications business etiquette program was the first etiquette program available online, and the company constantly researches the latest online training technology. Brody prepares for the future by listening to the concerns of her customers, and what she discovers helps her select new topics and methods to implement them (Brody, 2000).

Jan Magnuson, manager of customer information and administration for Discover Financial Services' training department, has also learned to flex for technology (Magnuson, 2000):

"Things happen and I've had to respond. New technologies such as laptop computers and the Internet have come along, and I've learned to teach these technologies, to incorporate them into our training methodology, and to tap dance when they decide not to work in the middle of a class."

One of my watershed experiences happened when, on a Friday, the organization decided to change the hardware vendor for a laptop computer rollout, yet wanted to go on with the planned training, using a new hardware supplier, that Sunday. There were people coming in from all over the country and we couldn't stop the rollout, so I asked our trainers to be flexible and our students to be patient.

The first two days of training became more demonstration than hands-on. We were up until 4 a.m. helping with the quality assurance testing of the new machines. Each week it got better. Finally, by the end of the fifth week, things were so calm they let me run the help desk!"

Training professionals have come to see technology as a natural extension of their training abilities and resources. They have learned to incorporate technology's strengths into the existing process of providing effective training. For example, they use computer-generated slides in appropriate presentations but not for interactive training when spontaneity and flexibility are needed. Do such slides serve the learner or do they set up a climate that is contrary to how people learn? The best trainers are flexible and able to incorporate Internet supplements, adapt training programs and methodologies, or lead learners in new systems with short turnaround times. The best trainers take into consideration all learning styles as they work with technology.

Throughout the last section of this book, you have been encouraged to help learners make commitments to learning, apply their new insights on the job, and participate in fruitful coaching. Although you cannot replace the dynamics of in-person classroom discussion or coaching, you can use technology in many ways to help learners apply their insights. For example, you can use the intranet and Internet for follow-up and commitment-making activities. Chatrooms and listserv discussions allow learners to share improvement ideas and concerns at will. You can also ask learners to read and research using the Web and to report back via email. Videoconferencing is a good way to handle additional meetings for troubleshooting and progress reporting. Learners can be guided to use technology-based communication productively and not to hide behind it.

In summary, technology has greatly affected how training is delivered and will continue to affect it throughout upcoming years. Be careful that you are not caught in the doldrums. Get help internally and externally with technological information so that you can meet the needs of today's learners.

DO YOU UNDERSTAND TODAY'S BUSINESS CLIMATE?

As a trainer, your knowledge of not only the customer's work but also the customer's general business climate is essential. You need to understand how the organization gets results within the current climate. Because you need to get learning results in that same environment, it matters to both of you.

The business climate changes daily for some industries, less often for others. Overall, an organization's intangible assets, such as the wisdom of its top executives or the loyalty of its customers, are becoming more valuable than its tangible assets, such as buildings and machines. Knowledge passes from one employee to another. In the United States, the number of mergers increased sixfold since 1986 from about 4,000 to about 25,000 (Abernathy et al., 1999). Change seems to be the only constant.

Trainers must be sensitive to the communication and training needs of employees working within a changing business climate. Initiate clear, frequent communication in a variety of formats to help learners prioritize and adjust. Encourage learners to communicate with each other in the same manner—frequently and with a variety of methods to adapt to co-workers' changing schedules, formats, and goals.

DO YOU RESPOND TO CHANGING WORKFORCE DEMOGRAPHICS?

The workforce has become a unique blend of younger and older workers. Senior employees are working in later years often on flexible or part-time schedules. They are not entering full retirement at what was the traditional retirement age. "Generation Xers" demonstrate an interest both in financial well-being and in progressive, open communication and equality (Conger, 1998b). Employees raised on the computer and the Internet (the net generation, or N-gen) demand more options, customization, and flexibility. Comfortable with teamwork and creativity, these N-gens are not impressed with meaningless theory and are alienated by outdated programs and materials.

Marjorie Brody has met the need for increased learner involvement and interaction by adding video clips to help learners visualize etiquette concepts; she also places the answers to in-class quizzes on the company Website. She responds to the N-gens' media orientation by commenting on and quoting from current media stars, including popular television characters. She asserts that young learners always perk up when she relates to their world by quoting current television stars (Brody, 2000).

The new generations still seek a balance of work and family. According to TalentAlliance, a not-for-profit business league of organizations, the dominant HR trend for future workers will remain ". . . to find meaningful work and to build lifelong careers that are productive and satisfying" (Abernathy et al., 1999). Constant access to the Internet promotes the 24-hour society; stores, cinemas, sports facilities, and public transportation will offer longer hours (World Future Society, 1998). Is your training available at any hour? Can you be flexible enough to help employees learn as they balance their work and family schedules?

In addition to addressing different generational learning needs, the leader must consider the overall work ethic. In a recent survey of 600,000 small employers, the National Federation of Independent Business discovered that 21 percent of employers complained about labor quality. For example, Lisa Dart, co-owner of Dart About Delivery, a New Orleans courier service, laments that many employees make just enough money to live on for a while and then stay home (Karr, 2000).

As a trainer, it may become more challenging for you to ask workers who are not even fully committed to the organization to commit to learning objectives. You will need to find ways to connect them closely to their personal and professional development. The changing patterns of work will continue to affect how adults learn. Have you considered what motivates this mix of employees as you design, deliver, and schedule your programs?

DO YOU MARKET AND NETWORK NONSTOP?

In the midst of ongoing change, corporate training and education are gaining respect often because of a shortage of qualified workers and positive management opinions about the importance of employee development. Even in a positive climate, it is important to communicate clearly how training aligns with strategic departmental and organizational goals. Not only do you need to learn the business climate, but you also need to take an active role in marketing your services or the services of your department.

How do you market? You have many choices. Marketing is an umbrella term for advertising, public relations, and marketing communications, which can include brochures, media appearances, articles, tapes, email, Internet notices, speeches, giveaways, telemarketing, surveys, free offers, and samples. Any marketing initiative is designed to communicate to your customers the wisdom and value of doing business with you. Many marketing tools can be used creatively to market training services.

Jan Magnuson, who promotes internal training to hundreds of Discover Card's employees, stresses the importance of marketing communications, "You just can't do it enough, and you have to find a way to make it noticeable. Everyone has tons of paper crossing his or her desk. We try to make ours noticeable by developing a look, a style, a logo, and a color. One sheet of colored paper stands out in those piles of white. It should also be useful, reader-friendly, extremely informative, and accurate. And, we've learned to time them well. If loads of paper land on people's desks on Monday morning, we get ours out for a Tuesday delivery" (Magnuson, 2000).

Though you will probably never see a word-of-mouth section in a marketing plan, this is one of the most powerful forms of communication and one of your cheapest marketing tools. Therefore, you should become adept at getting around and networking to position yourself and your department favorably within the organization. The ability to network is a critical skill. Let the rumor mill work for you rather than against you. As workers become more tied to their computers and telephones, you will need to find creative ways to get information to the right people.

Stan Piskorski, a 15-year sales training veteran at Corporate Dynamics, is known among his colleagues for nonstop networking. Piskorski (2000) describes his philosophy: "I can't know everything for my customers, but it is my job to know the menu of their potential interests so that I can investigate solutions and provide resources for them to use. The reason I go to meetings and network is that it helps me to listen better to the internal needs of my clients."

Frank Sonnenberg (1990) encourages networkers to develop not only strong ties, but weak ones as well, because ". . . weak ties expect less of you. They allow you to obtain access to people of diverse backgrounds and specialty areas. They serve as bridges to other groups of people, provide greater objectivity, and may approach a situation from an entirely different perspective."

In addition to circulating physically, you can also develop relationships with critical people who can help you build your network in other ways. For example, almost every major newspaper has either a career or workplace columnist. Become a fan of the column, and then develop a relationship with the columnist by occasionally responding to his or her articles via email. You may find yourself on the columnist's contributor list. This can result in some nice visibility for your organization and some publicity for yourself in the field of training and development.

You can attend training association meetings in your area to hear speakers who have researched, written, and spoken about leading trends. ASTD has chapters in nearly every major city in the country. The Society for Human Resource Professionals, the National Speakers Association, and the American Society of Sales Executives are a few more of the hundreds of relevant associations that you may want to visit.

It is also a good idea to stretch yourself and attend association meetings outside the field of training and development. You can serve as a sole resource for many people in other fields: engineers, publishers, computer experts, lawyers, accountants, real estate salespeople, and nurses. Consider attending chamber of commerce meetings, neighborhood or civic group events, parents' or singles' clubs, and sports-related events. Bring your business cards along, and be ready to describe your work and learn about others' work.

OUTSIDE THE BOX

I often used to present telephone service training. My expertise was in the areas of customer service, etiquette, and communication skills. I soon discovered that my clients wanted more telemarketing know-how. I happened to get a flyer about an American Telemarketing Association breakfast meeting in my area. I went and felt somewhat out of place as everyone else seemed to have an extensive call center background. That morning I met a woman who gave my name to a friend whom she had met via another healthcare association. That friend, Nancy Webster, now a partner with Care Education Group, a provider of healthcare training services, became one of my frequent clients and a long-time professional friend. Why? Initially, she simply didn't know anyone who did what I did. By stepping outside of my familiar training and development box, I not only increased my knowledge about telemarketing but also increased the visibility of my training services.—C.M.

HAVE YOU CONSIDERED REINVENTING YOUR ROLE?

With increased use of computer-based training, Web-based training, videoconferencing, and self-study programs, your training role is changing and will continue to change. For example, you will be increasingly involved with coaching learners and managers both. With learners, you will be called upon for just-in-time interventions, and you will be expected to be familiar with the technology that they are using.

As the workforce continues to shrink and good employees become even more valuable, you will be asked to help keep them in new ways. You may spend more time developing star employees or coaching employees in building a skill area that is holding them back. You may need to work more closely with HR specialists to link training objectives with specific job descriptions, rewards, and benefits.

If you are an independent training consultant, you will see increased demand for coaching, especially for star employees and executives who respond well to an outside point of view. Though you are probably accustomed to working in a variety of environments, you may use more virtual meetings or even meet in the client's home as the workplace becomes more flexible. Your media and presentation skills will become invaluable as programs become more accessible nationally and globally.

Both internal trainers and independent consultants will find themselves in consulting roles more often. Piskorski (2000) explains the trend with an interesting analogy: "These days, clients might think they want me to be a trainer, but I am most happy when my interaction with them ends up negating the need for training. Too many times, training is like taking an aspirin for a heart attack. It doesn't really solve the problem." Just as a healthy lifestyle prevents heart attacks, consultation and attention does solve most developmental problems eventually.

It is important to be ready to flex for your future role. You may love the change and challenge, or you may not like its new requirements. Remember, as Shakespeare wrote in *Hamlet*: "To thine own self be true, and it must follow, as the night, the day; thou canst not be false to any man." If your role begins to take on an uncomfortable aspect, give yourself permission to say so, to change, or even to get out. Trainers who are in a role that is not right for them are just not effective. It is important to reevaluate what you do. This book began by asking you to reflect on why you are a trainer. Do not forget to reconsider that question continually as you face the future. Self-assessment 13.1 will help you determine if you are flexed for the future.

WIDE-ANGLE VISION

The Futurist, a magazine devoted to trend watching and future thinking, can be an important resource for trainers. According to Wayne Burkan (1998), one of its contributors, if you want to be a trend watcher, you should use wide-angle vision: ". . . You should observe activity on the periphery of your everyday experience that may alert you to trends that will be important for you and your organization. This will allow you to act before a crisis happens." Wide-angle vision: What a great way for you to flex for the future!

Wide-angle vision will also help you see how to use your natural resources more clearly. This book has shown you the path to your natural resources, but it will take your own vision to maneuver that path. As a trainer, you lead learners down that path; you model the joy in discovery, the courage of self-reliance, and the articulation of insight. You partner with them on the path. You never lose them on the way. You play together in the spacious meadow of learning.

Our goal for this book has been to illuminate the natural, essential elements for building learning partnerships between trainers and learners. It is these natural elements that strengthen the heart in your training. This book is your guide and we hope you will return to the elements and exercises often to check your training heartbeat.

Self-Assessment 13-1.
Are you flexed for the future?

Directions: In summary, ask yourself the questions that this chapter has elicited about the future. Can you answer yes to all of them? Where do you need to flex your training muscles?

Question	Yes	No
Do you provide current or updated programs on a consistent basis?		
Do you acknowledge how technology has changed delivery and communications and use it in appropriate balance?		
Do you understand today's corporate climate with respect to your customer's business?		
Do you respond to changing workforce demographics in your industry?		
Do you market and network nonstop?		
Have you considered how your training role is changing and are you ready to reinvent it?		

▌ REFERENCES

Abernathy, D., H. Allerton, T. Barron, and J. Salopek. (1999, November). "Trendz." *Training & Development,* 24–41.

Adler, M. (1983). *How to Speak, How to Listen.* New York: Macmillan Publishing Company.

Ahlers, D. (1999, October). Letter to authors.

American Society for Training & Development. (1995, March). "What Motivates Trainers?" *Training & Development,* 15. Alexandria, VA: Author.

American Society for Training & Development. (1996, August). "Roles for Trainers." *Info-line,* 14. Alexandria, VA: Author.

Aubrey, R., and P.M. Cohen. (1995). *Working Wisdom: Timeless Skills and Vanguard Strategies for Learning Organizations.* San Francisco: Jossey-Bass.

Baker, B. (1999, July–August). "Can the Center Hold?" *Fast Company Magazine,* 124. Boston: Lowin Publishing.

Balu, R. (1999, December). "Whirlpool Gets Real with Customers." *Fast Company Magazine,* 74. Boston: Lowin Publishing.

Baron, E. (1995, July). "Tennis Anyone?" *Training & Development,* 15–19. Alexandria, VA: American Society for Training & Development.

Bassi, L.J., and M.E. Van Buren. (1999). *The 1999 ASTD State of the Industry Report.* Alexandria, VA: American Society for Training & Development.

Bellman, G.M. (1996). *Your Signature Path: Gaining New Perspectives on Life and Work.* San Francisco: Berrett-Koehler Publishers.

Bennis, W. (1989). *On Becoming a Leader.* Reading, MA: Addison-Wesley Publishing Company.

Bennis,W., and B. Nanus. (1985). *Leaders: The Strategies for Taking Charge.* New York: Harper & Row.

Blender, R. (1999, October). Letter to authors.

Brody, M. (2000, February 8). Telephone conversation with authors.

Brown, M.J. (2000, January 4). Email to authors.

Burkan, W. (1998, March). *The Futurist,* 35. Bethesda, MD: World Future Society.

Carr, C. (1990). *Front Line Customer Service.* New York: John Wiley and Sons.

Caudron, S. (1996, October). "Hire a Coach?" *Industry Week,* 87(3), 245.

Chang, R. (August, 1999). *The Passion Plan: A Step by Step Guide to Discovering, Developing, and Living Your Passion.* San Francisco: Jossey-Bass.

Conger, J.A. (1992). *Learning to Lead.* San Francisco: Jossey-Bass.

Conger, J.A. (1998a). *Winning 'Em Over: A New Model for Management in the Age of Persuasion.* New York: Simon & Schuster.

Conger, J.A. (1998b, First Quarter). "How Gen X Managers Manage." *Strategy & Business,* 25. New York: Booz-Allen & Hamilton.

Cooper, L., translator. (1932). *The Rhetoric of Aristotle..* Englewood Cliffs, NJ: Prentice-Hall.

Cougle, L. (1977). Conversation with the authors.

Covey, S.R. (1989). *The Seven Habits of Highly Effective People.* New York: Simon & Schuster.

Crain's Communications. (2000, February 7). "News You Can Use." *Crain's Chicago Business,* 2. Chicago: Author.

DePree, M. (1990). *Leadership is an Art.* New York: Dell Publishing.

Dixon, V., K. Conway, K. Ashley, and N. Stewart. (1995). *Training Competency Architecture.* Toronto: Ontario Society for Training & Development.

Drucker, P. (1999, October). "Beyond the Information Revolution." *The Atlantic Monthly,* 284(4), 47–57.

Ehrlich, E., and G.R. Hawes. (1984). *Speak for Success.* New York: Bantam Books.

Finnerty, M.F. (1996). "Coaching for Growth and Development." In *The ASTD Training & Development Handbook: A Guide to Human Resource Development,* R.L Craig, editor. New York: McGraw-Hill.

Firnstahl, T.W. (1989, July–August). "My Employees Are My Service Guarantee." *Harvard Business Review,* 89(4), 28–34.

Fox, D., V. Byrne and F. Rouault. (1999, August). "Performance Improvement: What to Keep in Mind." *Training & Development,* 40. Alexandria, VA: American Society for Training & Development.

Ghoshal, S., and C. Bartlett. (1999). *The Individualized Corporation: A Fundamentally New Approach to Management.* New York: HarperBusiness.

Gilman, C. (1997, May). Interview with authors.

Godfrey, N.S. (1999, October 1). Presentation to the Loyola University Women's Conference. Chicago.

Greenleaf, R.K. (1972). *The Institution as Servant.* Indianapolis, IN: Robert K. Greenleaf Center for Servant-Leadership.

Greenleaf, R.K. (1991). *The Servant as Leader.* Indianapolis, IN: Robert K. Greenleaf Center for Servant-Leadership.

Gumpert, D.E. (1986, July–August). "Growing Concerns: The Joys of Keeping the Company Small." *Harvard Business Review,* 6–7.

Haid, C. (2000, January). Letter to the authors.

Hammonds, K. (1999, November). "Hard Lives, Low Pay, Big Stakes." *Fast Company Magazine,* 96. Boston: Lowin Publishing.

Harrison, R. (1983). "Strategies for a New Age." In *The Leader-Manager,* J.N. Williamson, editor. New York: John Wiley & Sons.

Heck, D. (1997, January 2). Letter to the authors.

Heck, D. (1999, October 25). Letter to the authors.

Hickman, C.R., and M.A. Silva. (1984). *Creating Excellence.* New York: New American Library.

Hopper, D. (1997, May) Interview with authors.

Hupp, T. (1996, December 11). Letter to authors.

Impastato, L. (1999, October 15). Letter to authors.

Jackson, P., and H. Delehanty. (1995). *Sacred Hoops.* New York: Hyperion.

Karr, A.R. (2000, February 8). "Work Week." *The Wall Street Journal.*

Kelley, R. (1998). *How to be a Star at Work: Nine Breakthrough Strategies You Need to Succeed.* New York: Times Business.

Kennedy, D. (1984). *Super Natural Selling.* San Clemente, CA: Craig Publications.

Kennedy, M.M. (1999, June). "Managing Change: Demographics of the Evolving Workforce." Presentation to the Chicago Chapter, American Society for Training & Development. Chicago.

Knowles, M. (1995). *Designs for Adult Learning.* Alexandria, VA: American Society for Training & Development.

Kouzes, J.M., and B.Z. Posner. (1987). *The Leadership Challenge.* San Francisco: Jossey-Bass.

Lawson, K. (2000, February 23). Interview with authors.

Lee, D. (1996). "What Trainers Can Learn from Neuroscientists, Novelists, and Advertisers." *Performance in Practice.* Alexandria, VA: American Society for Training & Development.

Mackay, H. (1999, November 25). "Learning to Listen from Broadcaster Hugh Downs." *Minneapolis Star Tribune,* Section D, 2.

Magnuson, J. (2000, February 14). Letter to authors.

Malloy, T. (1999, December 2). Email letter to authors.

Maxson, A. (1999, October). Letter to authors.

McLagan, P. (1989). "HRD Work Outputs." *The Models.* Alexandria, VA: American Society for Training & Development.

McMurrer, D.P., M.E. Van Buren, and W.H. Woodwell, Jr. (2000, January). "Making the Commitment." *Training & Development,* 42. Alexandria, VA: American Society for Training & Development.

Meyering, S. (1999, November). Interview with authors.

Morris, B. (2000, February). "Executive Coaches: So You're a Player: Do You Need a Coach?" *Fortune,* 144.

O'Neill, M. (1996, August). "Dos and Don'ts for the New Trainer." *Info-line,* 13. Alexandria, VA: American Society for Training & Development.

Olesen, M. (1999, October). "What Makes Employees Stay." *Training & Development,* 49. Alexandria, VA: American Society for Training & Development.

Peters, T., and N. Austin. (1985). *A Passion for Excellence.* New York: Random House.

Pfeiffer, J.W., and A.C. Ballew. (1988). *Design Skills in Human Resource Development.* San Diego: University Associates.

Pink, D. (1999, September). "What Happened to Your Parachute?" *Fast Company Magazine,* 241. Boston: Lowin Publishing.

Piskorski, S. (2000, February 15). Interview with authors.

Prager, H. (1999, December). Interview with authors.

Prochnow, H. (1952). *1,001 Ways to Improve Your Conversation and Speeches.* New York: Harper & Brothers.

Robbins, D. (1990). "Trainees Know About Trainers." *Training & Development,* 34. Alexandria, VA: American Society for Training & Development.

Rogers, C. (1961). *On Becoming a Person.* Boston: Houghton Mifflin.

Rossotti, C. (1999, November). "What is the Best Use of Your Time?" *Fast Company Magazine,* 172. Boston: Lowin Publishing.

Rothwell, W. (1996). "Selecting and Developing the Professional HRD Staff." In *The ASTD Training & Development Handbook,* R.L. Craig, editor. Alexandria, VA: American Society for Training & Development.

Samusevich, M. (1999, December). Email to authors.

Sanborn, M. (1999, October 15). "e-Shifts for Professional Speakers." Presentation to the Professional Speakers of Illinois Chapter of the National Speakers Association. Oak Brook, IL.

Schueler, J. (2000, January). Interview with authors.

Senge, P.M. (1990). *The Fifth Discipline: The Art and Practice of the Learning Organization.* New York: Currency Doubleday.

Sheerer, R. (1999). *No More Blue Mondays.* Palo Alto, CA: Davies-Black Publishers.

Sonnenberg, F. (1990). *Marketing to Win.* New York: HarperBusiness.

Stadius, R., editor. (1999). *ASTD Trainer's Toolkit: Still More Needs Assessment Instruments.* Alexandria, VA: American Society for Training & Development.

Strauss, R. (1999, July–August). "Web Based Training." *Training Today,* 8. Chicago: Chicagoland Chapter American Society for Training & Development.

Suzuki, S. (1977). *Zen Mind, Beginner's Mind.* New York: Weatherhill.

Tuck, T.M. (2000, January). Interview with authors.

Waller, G. (1999, December). Interview with authors.

Waterman, R.H. (1987). *The Renewal Factor.* New York: Bantam Books.

Weidner, C.K. (1995, November 16). Interview with the authors.

Willin, J. (1996). Letter to authors.

World Future Society. (1998, April). *The Futurist,* 14. Bethesda, MD: Author.

Younger, S.M. (1993, June). "Learning Organizations: The Trainer's Role." *Info-line,* 7. Alexandria, VA: American Society for Training & Development.

Zaleznik, A. (1977, May–June). "Managers and Leaders: Are They Different?" *Harvard Business Review,* 55(4), 72.

ABOUT THE AUTHORS

BARRY LYERLY

Barry has a master's degree of arts in counselor education from the University of Iowa. As the former director of training at Marshall Field's in Chicago, he has trained and coached hundreds of people in a broad range of subjects, including presentation skills, leadership, team building, interpersonal effectiveness, and sales. His clients have included Crate & Barrel, Ace Hardware, Rockwell International, Bank of America, Lake Forest Hospital, and McDonald's Corporation.

Barry founded Lyerly Seminars in 1984. He has been a featured speaker for the Midwest Training Conference in Chicago, Illinois Hospital Association, Data Entry Managers Association, American Society for Training & Development International Conference & Exposition, and the Chicago Sales Training Association.

Barry has trained other trainers on his unique learning design, Insight to Action. Trainers who have benefited from this design include "professors" at McDonald's Hamburger University, internal and external facilitators at the University of Chicago Hospital's Academy, and HR professionals at the Bank of America.

CYNDI MAXEY

Cyndi earned her master's degree of arts in communication studies from Northwestern University at Evanston. She is now a speaker, trainer, and author who helps people fine-tune their speaking and listening skills. As the owner of Maxey Creative since 1989, she has developed and presented workshops internationally for such clients as Wendy's International, DARC Development Corporation, and Discover Financial Services.

She was a co-author for *The Communication Coach: Business Communication Tips from the Pro's,* a business communication anthology published by Coloring Outside the Lines in 1998. Her articles have appeared in several publications, including *Training & Development, Professional Speaker, Training Today, Business 2 Business Marketer,* and *Employment Relations Today.*

Cyndi, a certified speaking professional with the National Speakers Association, is a popular conference presenter on training and communication techniques. Active in the local and regional leadership of ASTD, she has won several ASTD-sponsored awards for service to the training field.